ALCTS Papers on Library Technical Services and Collections, no. 8

The Future of the Descriptive Cataloging Rules

Papers from the ALCTS Preconference,
AACR2000
American Library Association
Annual Conference
Chicago, June 22, 1995

edited by
Brian E. C. Schottlaender

series editor
Edward Swanson

American Library Association
Chicago and London 1998

Composition by the dotted i in Times and Helvetica Narrow on Xyvision

Printed on 50-pound white offset, a pH-neutral stock, and bound in 10-point coated cover stock by Data Reproductions Corp.

The paper used in this publication meets the minimum requirements of American National Standard for Information Sciences—Permanence of Paper for Printed Library Materials, ANSI Z39.48-1992. ∞

ISBN: 0-8389-3477-3

Copyright © 1998 by the American Library Association. All rights reserved except those which may be granted by Sections 107 and 108 of the Copyright Revision Act of 1976.

No copyright is claimed on "AACR and Authority Control" by Barbara Tillett, which the author wrote as part of her official duties as an employee of the U.S. government.

Printed in the United States of America.

02 01 00 99 98   5 4 3 2 1

Contents

Contributors to This Volume v

Toward the Future of the Descriptive
Cataloging Rules 1
Brian E. C. Schottlaender

Key Lessons of History: Revisiting the
Foundations of AACR 6
Lynne C. Howarth

AACR3? Not! 19
Michael Gorman

AACR and Authority Control 30
Barbara B. Tillett

Editions: Brainstorming for AACR2000 40
Martha M. Yee

What's Wrong with AACR2:
A Serials Perspective 66
Crystal Graham

Archival Description and New Paradigms
of Bibliographic Control and Access in the
Networked Digital Environment 84
Steven L. Hensen

Cataloging Uncertainty: Documents, Catalogs, and Digital Disorder   97
David M. Levy

Bibliographic Description and Digital Objects: Toward a New Discipline of Information Description and Management   107
Clifford Lynch

Bibliography   121

Acronyms and Initialisms Used   129

Index   131

Contributors to This Volume

Michael Gorman is Dean of Library Services at the Henry Madden Library, California State University, Fresno. From 1977 to 1988 he worked at the University of Illinois at Urbana-Champaign Library as, successively, Director of Technical Services, Director of General Services, and Acting University Librarian. From 1966 to 1977 he was, successively, head of cataloguing at the *British National Bibliography,* a member of the British Library Planning Secretariat, and head of the Office of Bibliographic Standards in the British Library. He has taught at library schools in his native Britain and in the United States.

Gorman is the first editor of the *Anglo-American Cataloguing Rules,* second edition, and its 1988 revision. He is the author of *The Concise AACR2;* editor of and contributor to *Technical Services Today and Tomorrow;* and editor of *Convergence,* the proceedings of the Second National LITA Conference. He is also the author of more than 100 articles in professional and scholarly journals.

Gorman is a Fellow of the Library Association and was the 1979 recipient of the Margaret Mann Citation and the 1992 recipient of the Melvil Dewey Medal. In 1997 he shared with Walt Crawford the ALCTS/Blackwell Scholarship Award for their book *Future Libraries: Dreams, Madness, and Reality* (Chicago: American Library Association, 1995).

Crystal Graham is currently head, Digital Information and Serials Cataloging at the University of California, San Diego. She began her professional career as the Associate CONSER Project Director at Cornell University. She also worked as serials cataloger at New York University and as Latin American studies monographs cataloger at UCSD before assuming her current position.

Graham has written widely on multiple versions and microform cataloging and is the author of the Association of Research Libraries *Guidelines for Bibliographic Records for Preservation Microform Masters.* She has served as the representative to the ALA Committee on Cataloging: Description and Access for both the ALCTS Serials Section and the ALCTS Reproduction of Library Materials Section. She also served as a member of the faculty of the ALCTS Serials Cataloging Institute.

Steven L. Hensen is Director of Planning and Project Development in the Special Collections Library at Duke University. He is the author of *Archives, Personal Papers, and Manuscripts,* the AACR2-based standard for archival cataloging, and of numerous articles and papers in the area of archival description and standards. In addition, he has conducted more than 40 workshops and consultancies in archival cataloging and the use of the MARC-AMC format.

Hensen has worked in special collections/archives at the State Historical Society of Wisconsin, the University of Chicago, Yale University, and the Library of Congress, and has served as Program Officer for Archives, Manuscripts, and Special Collections at the Research Libraries Group. He is a Fellow of the Society of American Archivists and is currently serving on its Governing Council. He was a member of the SAA National Information Systems Task Force and the Working Group on Standards for Archival Description. In 1995 Hensen was a member of the Bentley Library Fellowship team that developed an SGML-compliant encoding standard for archival finding aids. He continues to be active in developments relating to enhanced network access to archival information and collections.

Lynne C. Howarth is Dean of the Faculty of Information Studies, University of Toronto. Before joining the faculty of the University of Toronto, she worked at North York Public Library as a cataloging manager, a systems librarian, and an information network officer in public services. She has taught at McGill University; Ryerson Polytechnical University; and Seneca, Sheridan, and Georgian Colleges of Applied Arts and Technology.

Howarth's monograph publications include *A Brief Guide to AACR2, 1988 Revision, and Implications for Automated Systems* (co-authored with Jean Weihs), and the fifth and sixth editions of *AACR2 Decisions and Rule Interpretations*. She has several journal publications to her credit, including a four-part series in *Library Resources & Technical Services* entitled "AACR2R: Implementation and Use" (also co-authored with Jean Weihs). She is the recipient of two separate Social Sciences and Humanities Research Council of Canada grants in support of her research.

David Levy received his Ph.D. from Stanford in 1979 in computer science and artificial intelligence. He augmented that degree in 1982 with a diploma in calligraphy and bookbinding from the Roehampton Institute in London. A researcher at Xerox Palo Alto Research Center for the past decade, Levy has been much involved in the formation of a digital library research community. In 1995 he served as chair of the Digital Libraries Conference held in Austin, Texas.

Clifford Lynch is Executive Director of the Coalition for Networked Information and the former director of the University of California's Division of Library Automation where he was responsible for the UC MELVYL information system and network and for a variety of research and development projects. Lynch participates in several standards activities, including the NISO Standards Development Committee. He has published extensively and serves on a number of editorial boards. Lynch is a past president of the American Society for Information Science.

Brian E. C. Schottlaender is Associate University Librarian, Collections and Technical Services, at the University of California, Los Angeles. He served as chair of CC:DA during 1992-93 and is now the ALA representative to the Joint Steering Committee for Revision of AACR. Long active in standards-development for cataloging, Schottlaender currently directs and chairs both the Executive Council of the Program for Cooperative Cataloging and the CONSER Policy Committee. He is a member of the editorial boards of *Library Resources & Technical Services* and *Journal of Internet Cataloging.*

Barbara B. Tillett is the Chief of the Cataloging Policy and Support Office at the Library of Congress, in which capacity she also serves as the LC representative to the Joint Steering Committee for Revision of AACR. She has consulted widely on such issues as cataloging processes and organization, database design and record format, and authority control system specifications. She currently serves as a consultant to the IFLA Study Group on the Functional Requirements for Bibliographic Records and chairs both the IFLA Working Group on Form and Structure of Corporate Headings and the IFLA UBCIM Working Group on Minimal Data Elements for Authority Records and the ISADN.

Tillett has been active in ALA throughout her career, including founding the LITA/ALCTS Authority Control Interest Group in 1984. She has been chair of the ALCTS Cataloging and Classification Section and has served on the editorial and review boards of several publications, including *Cataloging and Classification Quarterly, Library Resources & Technical Services,* and *College & Research Libraries.* She has written extensively, with a focus on cataloging theory and practice, authority control, and library automation.

Martha M. Yee has been Cataloging Supervisor at the UCLA Film and Television Archive since 1983. She has long been an active member of ALA, including committee service on the ALCTS Audiovisual and Subject Analysis committees, MARBI, CC:DA, and the Executive Committee of the ALCTS Cataloging and Classification Section. She is currently chair of the Standards Subcommittee of the Cataloging and Documentation Committee of the Association of Moving Image Archivists and is a member of the Standing Committee on Standards of the Program for Cooperative Cataloging. Yee has published extensively on cataloging issues. In 1995 she received the ALCTS Best of LRTS Award for her publication "Manifestations and Near-Equivalents: Theory, with Special Attention to Moving-Image Materials."

Toward the Future of the Descriptive Cataloging Rules

Brian E. C. Schottlaender

This book is the product (or at least one of the products) of the AACR2000 Preconference sponsored by the ALCTS Cataloging and Classification Section, which was held in Chicago preceding the 1995 ALA Annual Conference. The preconference brought together eight presenters and almost 150 attendees with the same objective, "to subject the fundamental principles of the *Anglo-American Cataloguing Rules (AACR)* to a critical examination."[1]

The seed for the preconference was planted by John Duke when he and I attended the Workshop on Documenting Electronic Texts hosted by the Center for the Electronic Texts in the Humanities in 1994. Duke, then chair of the ALCTS Cataloging and Classification Section, was convinced that the time was right for a reconsideration of AACR. As I had just completed my tenure as chair of the ALA/ALCTS/CCS Committee on Cataloging: Description and Access, he encouraged me, and I agreed, to organize a conference that would afford the North American cataloging community a venue for taking a fresh look at the code.

Why the Need for a Critical Examination?

What were some of the circumstances that convinced Duke and me that the time was right for such a reconsideration? One of the first occurred quite some time ago—the second edition of the *Anglo-American Cataloguing*

Rules was still an infant—when the Library of Congress announced its decision not to implement chapter 11 for microforms. In the years since that very early departure from the code, there have been several similar partings of the ways. The archival community, as Steve Hensen notes, found AACR2 too "bookish," so it developed its own rules (APPM and RAD). The rare book community also was not taken with everything in AACR2— found it *insufficiently* bookish—and developed *its* own rules (DCRB, then BDRB). In the wake of the December 1989 Airlie House Forum on Multiple Versions, CC:DA decided to develop guidelines for the bibliographic description of reproductions and publish them *outside* the AACR2 framework because it wasn't clear how accommodating a framework AACR2 would prove to be. Likewise, CC:DA decided to issue guidelines for the bibliographic description of interactive multimedia outside the AACR2 framework, again in an effort to get a better sense of how accommodating AACR2 would be. Finally, the whole world seemed to be scrambling to apply some sort of order to the electronic revolution that, 20 or 30 years after we were warned it was coming, finally appeared to be here. Some were trying to use AACR2 to do so; many were not.

All this has led some of us to conclude that, although a good deal of what is in AACR2 continues to work, conceptually and practically, some of it no longer does. The AACR2000 Preconference, then, was a formal opportunity to review critically what works and what needs to be changed.[2]

What's Included:
An Overview of This Volume

The chapters that follow are all based on papers delivered at the preconference. The authors have revised them as necessary for publication and, occasionally, in order to include the most current developments in a particular area. I have reorganized the order of the papers fairly substantially from that followed during the preconference. My goal in doing so is to achieve a logical flow to their presentation such that the history and intent of the code are addressed first, its current shortcomings next, and its possible future—and that of descriptive cataloging generally—last.

In "Key Lessons of History: Revisiting the Foundations of AACR," Lynne Howarth traces the evolution of the principles that have guided code development from Panizzi and Cutter through Lubetzky and Verona. She reviews the development of the various editions and revisions of

AACR, concluding with the observation that AACR has a "pedigree" rather than a "lineage," that is, it has no common progenitor. She suggests that AACR can be considered only one of a series of "packaging devices" for identifying items as documents, and that it might come to function as a gateway to increasingly fine levels of bibliographic description. Michael Gorman in "AACR3? Not!" posits that there should be no AACR3 because AACR2 was itself misnamed (largely for political reasons) inasmuch as it really had very little in common with AACR. He argues not for revolutionary, structural change, but for evolutionary change within the structure and principles of AACR2, noting that any such changes have to be carried out within the "real-world context" of the code. Gorman concludes by describing several things that could or should be done to improve AACR2 without changing its structure and principles.

Barbara Tillett, in "AACR and Authority Control," traces the evolution of entries and references—and the uses thereof—from book catalogs through card catalogs to online catalogs, noting that, even in the online environment, most systems retain card-based models. She goes on to describe various conceptual models for conveying bibliographic relationships, including, most recently, that contained in the report of the IFLA Study Group on Functional Requirements for Bibliographic Records. She suggests that international authority records would be more useful were they transformed into "access control records" that document not just a single preferred form of an access point but all preferred forms of it as established by each participating country. In "Editions: Brainstorming for AACR2000," Martha Yee proposes a working definition for the word (and the concept) *edition,* namely "an item that is essentially the same work as another item, but with some differences significant to users." She then delineates several differences significant enough to warrant items being described in separate records and several others sufficiently less significant to be recorded on subrecords. Yee reviews current approaches to linking/collocating editions, noting that problems related to such linking/collocating "are rooted in our cataloging system as a whole, not just in AACR2." The primary issue, she observes, is not the creation of links, but rather the creation of links that are sharable, permanent, and ubiquitous. She concludes by suggesting specifications for an "ideal catalog system" that would address this issue.

Crystal Graham, in "What's Wrong with AACR2: A Serials Perspective," traces the ineffectiveness of AACR2 for serials cataloging to the code's cardinal principle (Rule 0.24), namely that ". . . the starting point for the description is the physical form of the item in hand." She notes that whereas Rule 0.24 suggests that seriality is a publication pattern that can apply to any material, the rest of the code does not follow through on that premise. She proceeds to describe several other weaknesses in AACR2 from the serials perspective, concluding that far greater savings in cataloging can be achieved by radical code revision than by incremental rule "tweaking." In "Archival Description and New Paradigms of Bibliographic Control and Access in the Networked Digital Environment," Steve Hensen states that the problem with the Paris Principles, and by extension with AACR2, for archival and manuscript materials is their focus on the description of physical items rather than on the information conveyed in those items. He suggests that this is problematic not only for the archival community but, increasingly, for the broader cataloging community as well. Hensen argues that two archival principles could have significantly wider and more useful applicability: first, that bibliographic records are used to facilitate *intellectual* access rather than *physical* control, and second, that bibliographic records are used as *an* access point, rather than *the* access point.

David Levy, in "Cataloging Uncertainty: Documents, Catalogs, and Digital Disorder," suggests that cataloging is concerned with more than "just" providing bibliographic access to materials. It is, rather, part of the system by which materials are created and maintained. Levy identifies five "loci of uncertainty" in the digital universe—materiality, boundaries, variability, permanence, and genre—and describes two information domains, primary and secondary. The primary domain includes books, journals, and so forth, while the secondary domain includes the range of surrogates (catalog records, URLs, etc.) that refer to, organize, and provide access to the materials in the former domain. He observes that the same uncertainties that obtain for digital materials in the former apply to digital surrogates in the latter. The issue, Levy concludes, is not the appearance of new digital genres, nor obtaining access to them, but, rather, their construction and maintenance and the institutions that attend to these activities. That is the context in which the future of cataloging must be assessed. Clifford Lynch closes out the volume with "Bibliographic Description and Digital Objects: Toward a New Discipline of Information Description and Management." Lynch observes that the environment in which we now find ourselves is characterized by mass-production cataloging to match mass-production publishing. Two overarching issues confront catalogers in this environment: changing user needs and the changing nature of information objects. In Lynch's opinion the use of the word *metadata* as a more fashionable synonym for descriptive cataloging misses the significance of current metadata developments. Traditional descriptive cataloging is just one of a range of approaches to describing information resources, a range that is itself only a part of the metadata range emerging as necessary to manage digital resources. "Full-quality" cataloging now coexists with cataloging based on simpler schemes. The challenge, in Lynch's view, lies in integrating the varying approaches to exercising control over digital content.

Conclusion

Several themes emerge from the papers that make up this volume. The first is that distinctions in the environment in which we currently find ourselves are getting finer. The boundaries between edition, version, and format, between description and access, between an item and the record that describes it, are no longer as clear as they once were. Second, although standards continue to be important, consensus is growing that we should concentrate our efforts in this arena on things that matter and accept variability among those that don't. Third, there is an emerging view that bibliographic control is an iterative or accretive process, what Hensen refers to as a "hierarchy of surrogacy." Fourth, the emphasis of AACR2 on describing the physical attributes of an item rather than its intellectual content is increasingly problematic. Fifth, the focus of bibliographic description, it seems, should be on significant differences between bibliographic entities, what Graham refers to as "intentional" differences and what Yee labels "differences significant to users." Finally, there is growing conviction that AACR2 is inadequate to the task of describing the increasing complexity of relationships between bibliographic entities.

In closing, I want to thank the authors for their outstanding contributions, the individuals who helped me plan and organize the event, the ALCTS office staff for their invaluable assistance, John Duke for having the idea in the first place, and, finally, Sherri for everything always. Neither the preconference nor this book would have come to pass without them.

Notes

1. Brochure for ALCTS Preconferences to the ALA Annual Conference, June 22–23, 1995, Chicago, Illinois.
2. There had been an earlier, informal opportunity, organized by Laurel Jizba (of Michigan State University) during the ALA Midwinter Meeting in Los Angeles in February 1994. *See* "Future Directions for the Cataloging Rules Meeting" in the Bibliography.

Key Lessons of History: Revisiting the Foundations of AACR

Lynne C. Howarth

It is perhaps fitting that a Canadian revisit the foundations of the Anglo-American Cataloguing Rules. A good part of Canada's history as a nation derives from its initial status as a colony of Great Britain. Canadians have a historic affinity with the Anglo perspective. However, our physical adjacency to the United States, and concomitantly close economic, political, and social ties, also give Canadians a somewhat intimate, if not always comfortable, acquaintance with the American point of view. In addition to straddling the Anglo and American positions, which is indeed what AACR has endeavored to do across time, I also will try to mediate between the past and the future from the perspective of the present. I intend to revisit the principles and objectives of AACR as they have been articulated by cataloguing theorists and as presented in individual editions of AACR over time. I briefly will examine and evaluate how AACR has evolved, focusing on particular changes that have occurred from one edition to the next. With this framework having been set, I then will identify what I refer to as the key lessons of history, using these as the springboard for some predictions about the future of AACR.

In his now legendary rejoinder to the Right Hon. the Earl of Ellesmere and the other commissioners appointed to inquire into the constitution and government of the British Museum, Sir Anthony Panizzi vindicated his discontinuation of the compilation of the *British Museum Catalogue* after publication of only one volume with such persuasive arguments as the following:

I trust, my Lord, that you will agree with me that no catalogue of a large public library . . . can be called 'useful' in the proper sense of the word, but one in which the title are [sic] both 'accurate', and so 'full' as to afford all that information respecting the real contents, state, and consequent usefulness of the book which enable a reader to choose, from among many editions, or many copies, that which may best satisfy his wants, whether in a literary or scientific, or in a bibliographical point of view.[1]

Although not explicitly stated as principles or objectives, Panizzi's description of the nature and content of an alphabetical catalogue can be seen as a recurring theme throughout the almost 150 years of code development predating our deliberations today. The notions of "useful," "accurate," and "full" resurface, although somewhat altered, in Charles Cutter's four editions of *Rules for a Dictionary Catalog*. Cutter's interpretation of "usefulness" is perhaps best expressed in his phrase "for the convenience of the public," an overriding principle that could compromise, in some instances, "strict consistency in a rule and uniformity in its application." While his rules were intended to be user-centered in their interpretation and application, Cutter also acknowledged the operating realities of libraries, recognizing that "[n]o code of cataloging could be adopted in all points by everyone, because the libraries for study and the libraries for reading have different objects, and those which combine the two must do so in different proportions."[2] Panizzi's "useful" and "full" are given shape and further defined within Cutter's categories of short-title, medium-title, and full-title or bibliographic catalogues. These categories will be revisited shortly.

The *Rules for a Dictionary Catalog* made explicit certain underlying principles and objectives. Cutter's three "objects" for a dictionary catalogue were as follows:

1. To enable a person to find a book of which either
the author
the title   } is known.
the subject
2. To show what the library has
by a given author
on a given subject
in a given kind of literature.
3. To assist in the choice of a book
as to its edition (bibliographically)
as to its character (literary or topical).[3]

Seventy years passed before another set of objectives was formally documented in the library literature. With the second preliminary edition of the 1908 *A.L.A. Catalog Rules* having just been published and roundly criticized, and responding to Andrew Osborn's 1941 paper, "The Crisis in Cataloging," Seymour Lubetzky articulated general principles that were to underlie the code of rules for the description of books in the Library of Congress. He suggested that the functions of descriptive cataloguing were:

1. To describe the significant features of the book which will serve (a) to distinguish it from other books and other editions of this book, and (b) characterize its content, scope, and bibliographical relations;
2. To present the data in an entry which will (a) fit well with the entries of other books and other editions of this book in the catalog, and (b) respond best to the interests of the majority of readers.[4]

Based on these two functions, six principles were derived relating to (1) the terms of description (essentially those used on the title page or elsewhere in the book); (2) the extent of the description ("as fully as necessary for the accepted functions, but with an economy of data, words, and expression"—or, as I interpret it, as full as necessary, but not necessarily full); (3) the organization of the elements of description ("in such order as will best respond to the normal approach of the reader and will be suited for integration of the entry with the entries of other books and editions in the catalog"); (4) the integration of these elements ("All information relating to a given bibliographical term should be integrated, except where the length or construction of a given statement makes its integration with the other data undesirable. In this case the statement may preferably be given in a note."); (5) identification of sources of data; and (6) capitalization, punctuation, and accents.[5]

In Lubetzky's principles can be found the recurring themes of "usefulness" and "fullness," and a user-centered approach that, while apparent, is more subdued than that of Cutter's "convenience of the public." The functions and principles contained in this 1946 Library of Congress publication were an attempt to simplify what Osborn had characterized as "legalistic" and "perfectionist" approaches to cataloguing, to strike a sensible balance between uniform standards and the differing needs of various types of libraries, and, in Lubetzky's words, "to give our code direction, coherence, and logical construction; and also to provide the cataloger with general guidance in meeting the numerous cases which cannot be specifically provided for in the rules."[6]

The kind of soul-searching debate that preceded the publication of the 1949 *Rules for Descriptive Cataloging* spilled over into considerations of rules for author and title entries, and particularly for choice and form of the main entry. Two key players in the discussion of the function of main entry in library catalogues were Eva Verona and Seymour Lubetzky. In his review of the working papers on the function of the main entry in the alphabetical catalogue, submitted to the International Conference on Cataloguing Principles, Paris, 1961, Leonard Jolley summarized the essential differences in the debate:

> Lubetzky and Verona agree on the three functions of the catalogue but they do not assess their importance in the same way. Verona puts the functions in the accepted way: it is the function of the catalogue to answer three questions: (1) is this particular book in the library? (2) which editions of this particular book are in the library? (3) which books by this author are in the library? Lubetzky formulates the same position rather differently: it is the function of the catalogue: (1) to show whether the library has a particular item, issued under a certain name of the author or a certain title, and (2) to identify the author and the work represented by the item and to relate the various works of the author and various editions and translations of the work. He holds strongly to the view that the second objective is essential to the basic purpose of the catalogue, which is to enable a user to determine with certainty whether or not a library has a particular work and to select the copy of the work which will best serve his purpose.
>
> Verona considers that the catalogue should place first the needs of the great majority of readers and holds that the majority of readers are primarily interested in tracing a particular item, which will most often be a recent publication. This is clearly a very important difference of emphasis.
>
> There is another important difference in that Lubetzky argues almost exclusively from principles and only once ... deviates into expediency. Verona is constantly urging the claims of expediency.[7]

Jolley concludes that although Lubetzky argues convincingly that entry under the title found in the publication itself impairs the usefulness of the catalogue, his own proposal to always enter under the original title or an accepted conventional title ignores the extent of bibliographic information readily available to catalogue users, is often unworkable in application, and is therefore unacceptable.

Revised Objectives

The revised objectives or "Functions of the Catalogue" that finally emerged as part of the "Paris Principles" read as follows:

> The catalogue should be an efficient instrument for ascertaining:
>
> 2.1 whether the library contains a particular book specified by
> (a) its author or title, *or*
> (b) if the author is not named in the book, its title alone, *or*
> (c) if the author and title are inappropriate or insufficient for identification, a suitable substitute for the title; and
>
> 2.2 (a) which works by a particular author *and*
> (b) which editions of a particular work are in the library.[8]

The two cataloguing principles resulting from the Paris conference essentially mirror the first two of Cutter's three "objects," while the third—namely, "to assist [the catalogue user] in the choice of the book"—is nowhere explicit. It might be argued that Cutter's third object is implied in the phrase "an efficient instrument for ascertaining," though one might well ask, "ascertained by whom?" As information systems designers are aware, bibliographic content and displays for professional intermediaries can differ quite significantly from those for public users.

Anglo-American Cataloguing Rules

Having reviewed some key sets of principles or objectives articulated by cataloguing theorists, I should like to now "fast forward" to the actual Anglo-American Cataloguing Rules, the first edition of which was issued in 1967. This was yet another code in whose drafting Lubetzky played a prominent role, and one for which the American—or in this case, the North American—and British texts were issued separately. As the Introduction to AACR1 indicates, the "Statement of Principles" adopted by the International Conference on Cataloguing Principles in 1961 provided the underlying framework for the rules. Nonetheless, economic and institutional realities intervened and certain provisions of the Paris Principles were modified to accommodate operational requirements of the Library of Congress and member institutions of the Association of Research Libraries concerned with the potential high costs of retrospectively converting entries to conform with the new rules.

The most significant departure of AACR1 from the Paris Principles was the continuation of entry of certain types of corporate bodies indirectly under place name, rather than directly under the name of the body itself. AACR1 also differed in fundamental approach from its predecessors. Whereas previous codes emphasized specific rules for various types of publications and for different classes of persons and corporate bodies, the 1967 code was based on a set of principles—the Paris Principles—to be followed "as consistently as possible, allowing for the necessity of reaching common agreement, and, in certain cases, of coming to terms with economic imperatives."[9] It is in this extension of general rules to specific cases that we observe Lubetzky's influence. Although earlier codes had the advantage of providing answers to specific questions in one place, they were less amenable to generalization in resolving bibliographic problems that did not fit neatly in one category or another. In those instances, a series of ad hoc decisions based on "cataloguing by analogy" resulted. As the introduction to AACR1 concludes, "Apart from operational difficulties, this case-by-case approach to the development of rules tended to obscure underlying principles and basic system [sic] while opening the way to the inclusion of many exceptions and inconsistencies. The result was necessarily detrimental to the effectiveness of the catalog as a finding tool."[10] When all was said and done, however, AACR1 remained, as indeed it portrayed itself to be, a set of rules primarily oriented to general research libraries, with public libraries playing a decidedly secondary role. Where the needs of research libraries and other types of libraries were irreconcilable, alternative rules were provided for the latter.[11]

AACR1 was designed to meet the requirements of multiple-entry alphabetic catalogues in which all entries for persons or corporate bodies appeared under a uniform title or were related by references. Nonetheless, it maintained the distinction between main and added entries, arguing that, even in multiple-entry catalogues where a unit card or master record was created with the same descriptive information for each entry, "it sometimes happens that a work other than the work being cataloged, must be identified by a single entry—e.g., a work about which the work in hand has been written or a work on which the work in hand has been based."[12] Moreover, AACR1 supported a standard mode of identifying bibliographic entities in single-entry bibliographies, book lists, bibliographical citations, order lists, and so on, following, in the words of the code, "the principle firmly established in modern cataloging and bibliography, that a work should be specified by its author and title or, if it lacks an author, by its title."[13]

AACR2

The second edition of the Anglo-American Cataloguing Rules, published in 1978, accomplished as one of its objectives the reconciliation of the British and North American versions in one text. While the preface to AACR2 confessed to having the same principles and underlying objectives as the first edition, and to "being firmly based on the achievement of those who created the work first published in 1967,"[14] it departed in major, and sometimes radical, ways from AACR1. Evolutionary in its development, AACR2 was revolutionary in its presentation and initial impact. For one thing, the rules were designed "for use in the construction of catalogues and other lists in general libraries of all sizes."[15] Moreover, whereas AACR1 provided guidelines for research libraries, with alternative rules in some cases for other types of "non-research" libraries, AACR2 did almost the opposite. The General Introduction cautions "specialist and archival libraries" to use the rules as the basis for their cataloguing and to augment their provisions, as required. In short,

> The rules cover the description and entry of all library materials commonly collected at the present time, and the integrated structure of the text will facilitate the use of the general rules as a basis for cataloguing uncommonly collected materials of all kinds and library materials yet known.[16]

Contrary to earlier codes, but consistent with AACR1 and carrying further its commitment to having general rules that could be applied consistently to specific cases, AACR2 was structured such that rules moved along a continuum from general to specific with references from the latter back to the former. This layout underlines a further attempt to discourage "legalistic," case-by-case approaches to cataloguing, though the subsequent proliferation of Library of Congress Rule Interpretations has undermined, in practical terms, the AACR2 intent to allow for generalizable and flexible application of the rules.

In deciding on policy questions or new proposals, the Joint Steering Committee for Revision of AACR was informed by the following guidelines:

1. Maintenance of general conformity with the Paris Principles, *as manifested in the first edition* [emphasis added];

2. Particular attention to developments in the machine processing of bibliographic records;
3. Continuance of the ISBD(M) as a basis for the bibliographic description of monographs, and commitment to the principle of standardization in the bibliographic description of all types of materials;
4. Determination of the treatment of non-book materials primarily from a consideration of the published cataloguing rules of the Canadian Library Association, the Library Association, the Association for Educational Communications and Technology; and of the ALA revision of chapter 12 of the 1967 text.[17]

As regards the first guideline, AACR2 did not simply *preserve* those Paris Principles "manifested in the first edition"; rather, it *extended* the Principles. The AACR1 practice of entry under the name of a place for certain institutional bodies, for example, was abandoned. Likewise, AACR2 discontinued form subheadings in favor of uniform titles under names of states or other territorial authority for constitutions, laws, and treaties, and certain other similar works, and thus better conformed to Paris Principle 9.5. As the Preface suggests, the JSC was not unaware of the potential difficulties and costs that might be incurred by larger research libraries attempting retrospective conversion of existing entries to the 1978 standards. But, as Peter Lewis, chair of the JSC, explained:

> with the increased flexibility of modern systems for processing bibliographic data and of catalogue formats, the inertia of the retrospective file is much less than it has been in the past. Many of the larger research libraries have, or may expect soon to have, the capability of relatively inexpensive conversion of at least part of their catalogues to more flexible forms of storage; and, too, there appears generally a much wider acceptance in libraries of the propriety and utility of simply closing old catalogues when they become too large to respond easily to new requirements of their users and starting new ones alongside them.[18]

In the opinion of the authors of AACR2, the "single most important contribution to meeting the needs of machine processing" (i.e., guideline 2) was "in the achievement of an integrated and standardized framework for the systematic description of all library materials, as presented by Part I."[19] This was also viewed as a major step along the road to developing a truly international cataloguing code. Conformity to ISBD(G) and the multinational, multiorganizational collaboration involved in adopting it as a general framework for description also signaled a commitment by the Anglo-American cataloguing community to the principle of universal bibliographic control.

AACR2 was unique among all its predecessors in introducing descriptive cataloguing as the primary activity in the creation of the bibliographic record. "Primary," in this instance, refers to first in sequence as well as to principal in importance. Whereas previous codes had included rules for the choice and form of entries before those for describing various types and formats of material, AACR2 set out the eight areas of description for book and various nonbook items in part I, to precede "Headings, Uniform Titles, and References" in part II. AACR2 also introduced the concept of three levels of description, which, in my opinion, are somewhat reminiscent of Cutter's "short-title, medium-title, and full-title" categories for catalogues. Levels one, two, and three afforded cataloguers and cataloguing agencies the flexibility to create descriptive records of minimal, medium, or detailed length, depending upon such factors as the nature of the material, its relative use or shelf life, the size or value of the collection, the capabilities of automated systems used for storing and displaying the record, and the availability of resources for actual cataloguing operations.

The code also included "alternative rules," "optional additions," and other rules or parts of rules designated by the word "optionally." As Rule 0.7 explains:

> These provisions arise from the recognition that different solutions to a problem and differing levels of detail and specificity are appropriate in different contexts. Some alternatives and options should be decided as a matter of cataloguing policy for a particular catalogue or bibliographic agency and should therefore be exercised either always or never. Other alternatives and options should be exercised case by case.[20]

The Introduction continues with a recommendation that all cataloguing agencies differentiate between these two types of alternatives and options and keep a record of their policy decisions and of the conditions under which a particular option will be applied. The inclusion of these alternatives and options sparked a proliferation of decisions and rule interpretations from the Library of Congress and national cataloguing agencies in Canada, the United Kingdom, and Australia, as cataloguers sought guidance as to which bibliographic routes to follow.

The 1988 revision of AACR2 was intended to address some of the problems and shortcomings of the second edition. It offered new rules

(1) for bibliographic situations that lacked rules, (2) for new media, and (3) for new general material designations. It corrected publishing errors and examples and refined rules for materials for the visually impaired and for media that had changed technologically since 1978.

The revised code largely eliminated options in access points, while increasing the possibilities for descriptive cataloguing. It further emphasized ease of use through the rearrangement of some rules, the addition of examples, and the revision of wording and numbering for consistency and clarity. It also provided for the omission of standard information that would itself contribute to shortening the length of bibliographic records —a consequence viewed as necessary for minimizing the expense of storing machine-readable records in increasingly large databases.

Although these changes were not insubstantial, they focused on refining and clarifying the code, and were nowhere viewed in the sometimes cataclysmic terms reserved for the 1978 code. With the issuing of the 1993 amendments, peace was largely restored to the land of bibliographic control! At least until now. . . .

In Retrospect

After more than a century of code development and revision, what are the key lessons of bibliographic history that we can derive and from which we may benefit as we contemplate the future of the Anglo-American Cataloguing Rules? In the first place, AACR can be characterized as having a "pedigree" rather than a "lineage." The latter is indicative of a linear descent from a common progenitor, whereas a "pedigree" is a record of a line of ancestors. AACR has no one "common progenitor"; it is the composite of a line of bibliographic ancestors, reflecting influences from such individual cataloguing theorists and practitioners as Panizzi and Cutter, from such institutions as the Library of Congress and national cataloguing agencies, and from such organizations as the American Library Association and its counterparts in Canada, the United Kingdom, and other parts of the world through IFLA. The diversity of AACR's ancestry is a part of its strength.

AACR's genealogy has given it the flexibility to respond to changes in the bibliographic landscape across the decades. In that sense AACR has been essentially reactive, rather than proactive, in addressing change. Various types of print and nonprint materials have come and gone; libraries and other information services have moved from manual to increasingly automated operational environments, aided by MARC—AACR's cousin for record communication; client types and needs have expanded and diversified in an increasingly sophisticated manner as users have become more bibliographically and computer literate. Today's reality includes not only numerous electronic databases in the form of online public access catalogues, online bibliographic citations and full text (Dialog, Medline, etc.), and networked CD-ROM databases, but also that vast and prolific information resource, the Internet. It is a bibliographic reality that has caused cataloguers to question the continued existence, let alone the relevance, of AACR.

Questions surrounding the necessity for main entry, or whether the code should treat an item as a bibliographic unit or as a literary work, seem to pale when the whole *raison d'être* for the surrogate is under scrutiny. Why, when a searcher can access a full document through a front-end search engine such as Netscape, or can glean the format and content of an electronic publication through the TEI header attached to an SGML-encoded document, is there a need for AACR? Perhaps it is becoming quickly obsolete, or at least anachronistic.

I think it no surprise that the number of discussions concerning the continued viability of a code for description and access have increased dramatically over the past three to five years, nationally and internationally. Nor do I think it unexpected that front-line cataloguers are becoming increasingly restive and vocal about the perceived inadequacies of the bibliographic code. AUTOCAT, TSIG-L, Intercat, and the more recent CC:DA list brim with calls for change from a generation of cataloguers who have instant access to one another via e-mail, electronic bulletin boards, and Internet information sources, and who have cut their cataloguing teeth on a code—AACR2—that encourages practitioner discretion, flexibility through descriptive record levels, choice through the mechanism of options, and an overall tone that supports decisions based on internal agency policy and operational constraints. Although it has always benefited from a considerable amount of external input, AACR has evolved into an increasingly "democratic" code that, by its nature, invites the opinions and participation of the "common cataloguing folk." While such cooperative interaction is laudable, a danger exists that too many voices will contribute to a code that begins to exhibit the too-familiar characteristics of "legalistic perfectionism," to invoke Andrew Osborn. In their impatience to alter and shape a bibliographic code that responds much more quickly than at present to a world of rapid change, cataloguers may lose sight of AACR's original objectives as articulated by

Charles Cutter: a simple yet elegant framework that stresses the convenience of the public while remaining sensitive to operational realities and administrative constraints. It may also be helpful, indeed necessary, for us to revisit and perhaps define or refine Panizzi's objectives for "useful," "accurate," and "full" catalogue records.

The so-called information explosion has made it even more imperative that we consider the merits of AACR as a "packaging" device capable of informing clients as to the nature, content, format, potential use, and availability of documents. I suggest that AACR should be considered one element within a series of packaging devices, serving to identify composite items or documents, rather than necessarily discrete parts of items or documents. The code can be used to create surrogates at the metadata level of the information chain. In AACR we have the essential framework for a "front-end" tool, a kind of meta-surrogate that could serve as a gateway to discrete parts of an item. Once a searcher has located a record for an item, he or she could then be linked to the TEI header for more detail concerning the parts of the item or other related elements. In a sense, I envision a kind of *Rules for Archival Description* that provides for an increasingly detailed and hierarchically structured series of records, all linked successively.

In times of rapid change, it is sometimes hard to resist "worst-case scenario" predictions. Yet when the future becomes the past, it is seldom revolution, but evolution that prevails. I believe that we are at another exciting crossroad for the evolution of AACR, at the beginning of a new world order for bibliographic control. We have heard a great deal about creating records that link and relate items, concepts that strike me as largely mechanical adjustments in increasingly computerized environments. AACR's inherently strong and flexible character places it in a position of remaining a viable packaging tool, or, in Eric de Grolier's words, a "switching device" that will propel the code along the information superhighway.

Notes

1. Sir Anthony Panizzi, "Mr. Panizzi to the Right Hon. the Earl of Ellesmere.—British Museum, January 29, 1848," in *Foundations of Cataloging: A Sourcebook,* Michael Carpenter and Elaine Svenonius, eds. (Littleton, Colo.: Libraries Unlimited, 1985), 21.
2. Charles A. Cutter, *Rules for a Dictionary Catalog,* 4th ed., rewritten (Washington, D.C.: Government Printing Office, 1904), 11.
3. Ibid.

4. Seymour Lubetzky, "Principles of Descriptive Cataloging," in *Foundations of Cataloging*, 106.
5. Ibid., 107.
6. Ibid.
7. Leonard Jolley, "The Function of the Main Entry in the Alphabetical Catalogue; A Study of the Views Put Forward by Lubetzky and Verona," in International Federation of Library Associations, *International Conference on Cataloguing Principles, Paris, 9th–18th October, 1961: Report*, A. H. Chaplin and Dorothy Anderson, eds. (London: Clive Bingley on behalf of IFLA, 1969, c1963), 159–60.
8. "Statement of Principles, International Conference on Cataloguing Principles, Paris, October 1961," in *Foundations of Cataloging*, 179.
9. *Anglo-American Cataloging Rules*, North American Text (Chicago: American Library Association, 1967), 5 (hereafter cited as *AACR*).
10. *AACR*, 5.
11. *AACR*, 1.
12. *AACR*, 2.
13. Ibid.
14. *Anglo-American Cataloguing Rules*, 2d ed. (Chicago: American Library Association, 1978), v (hereafter cited as *AACR2*).
15. *AACR2*, 1.
16. Ibid.
17. *AACR2*, vii.
18. *AACR2*, x.
19. *AACR2*, viii.
20. *AACR2*, 2–3.

AACR3? Not!

Michael Gorman

The Larger Context

Before I discuss AACR and its future, I would like to spend a little time on the wider context—the future of libraries and human communication and the importance of bibliographic standards.

Will There Be Libraries?

Yes, libraries will continue to exist, for two reasons at least. First, libraries have the eternal mission of identifying, acquiring, preserving, organizing, and providing access to recorded knowledge, information, and data in all forms, and of providing instruction and assistance in their use. There is no reason to believe that this mission will change. Second, no evidence exists that, for the first time in human history, one form of communication will obliterate all other forms: that is, that we are looking at an all-wired, all-electronic future. Most advances in human communication have been accompanied by predictions that they would wipe out what preceded them; however, none of the latter has ever died. One can imagine those who first impressed triangular marks on clay chortling over the imminent demise of the stone-carving industry, but we still mark the tragedy of Vietnam in inscribed stone. The truth is that each form of communication has its own strengths: In the particular case that occupies us today, electronic communication is unparalleled in communicating information and data, and print on paper is unsurpassed as a medium for sustained reading leading to the acquisition of knowledge.

Not only will libraries exist, but those libraries will be places and not just ideas. Those places will store and give access to "traditional" collections, will provide access to electronic resources, will provide assistance and instruction in the use of all kinds of recorded knowledge and information, and will continue to be social institutions of great value to the community, university, school, corporation, or other assemblage of human beings that they serve.

Do We Need Standards?

One of the greatest names in modern librarianship is that of Fred Kilgour, the founder of OCLC, possibly the most important advance ever in library cooperation. I have worked with a few such "great persons" and known others and can testify that their professional lives are characterized by single-mindedness and the sort of drive that is not content until their Great Idea—the one shining thing that separates them from mere mortals—is brought to fruition. Kilgour's Great Idea, OCLC, arose from humble beginnings—a few college libraries in Ohio—to become the nearest thing to a universal bibliography we have ever seen, a force that has revolutionized the organization and economics of almost every library in this country and the single force that has made bibliographic standardization central and necessary. After all, what would OCLC have become if it had not surmounted the standardization difficulties of its early years? To be accepted, OCLC had to embrace MARC, AACR2, LCSH, LCC, and DDC. It must be admitted that some of the embraces were given more willingly than others, but it cannot be denied that standardization—bibliographic quality, if you like—was the framework within which OCLC succeeded or that the impetus behind the great advances made in bibliographic standardization in recent years was, in great measure, due to OCLC and the general growth in cooperation.

All that being said, how sad it is to read Fred Kilgour writing in the *Journal of the American Society for Information Science* about some "research" that he has been pursuing purporting to show that searching by the surname of the author, the first word of the title, and the last word of the title will produce 20 or fewer entries 92 percent of the time. He then goes on to make the leap that this "finding" will enable libraries to eliminate what he is pleased to call "manual descriptive cataloging" and that we should implement "keyword known-item OPACs" to replace the "traditional bibliographic segment" of current OPACs.[1] The danger is that this tosh, coming from so substantial a source, may be used by administrators to destroy a central part of the library enterprise, the bibliographic structure and organization upon which we depend to serve the library's users.

Can We Incorporate Electronic Resources into the Bibliographic Structure?

> A wealth of scientific information exists on the Internet. Finding and understanding this information remains a problem, though.
> —Blurb from a conference program

> The libraries of tomorrow are being shaped around a vision that once seemed futuristic. Librarians, Internet resources, and the digital library will be interwoven into a network of human and electronic resources.
> —Blurb from another conference program

No clear answer exists regarding whether we can incorporate electronic resources into the bibliographic structure. So the answer becomes, well, yes . . . maybe. The first of the preceding quotations has at least the merit of honesty. In what must be a contender for understatement of the year, it acknowledges that the problem of locating "information" in the chaos that we call the Internet is not easily resolved. Moreover, once located, said "information" will, in most cases, lack provenance, authority, organization, completeness, and the other attributes that we have come to expect of recorded knowledge, information, and data. The second quotation is mere hand waving. It states with confidence something that is unsupported by facts and insupportable as an idea. The same "idea" has been written confidently a zillion times by now, so it must be true—right? Wrong. The reasons why are many but I would like here to concentrate on the problem of finding and using Internet resources.

The Net is the moral equivalent of a huge library in which all the books have been piled higgledy-piggledy after being wrenched from their bindings and having their indexes and front matter removed. There are souls—dedicated serendipitists with time on their hands—who would enjoy spending hours searching in this vandalized library for meaningful clumps of text and pictures without bothering about whence they came or which human mind created them. With a bit of luck, there would be some clues in the torn pages that would help these "early surfers" make a sort of sense out of what they had found. The Net surfer has, of course, even more fun. There is the added excitement of being able to add to, delete, alter, distort, or do what they will with the found "information" before sending it out again into the chaos for the delectation of their fellow surfers. More, there is the thrill of uncertainty about whether the shards of texts and pictures that they find are what they say they are and were issued by the persons whose names are attached.

It must be difficult for the futurists who believe in the "interweaving of human and electronic resources" to come to terms with the fact that pre-electronic humans—particularly those humans called writers, publishers, and librarians—have devised intricate and highly effective methods for locating, identifying, and making usable complex accumulations of recorded knowledge, information, and data. It is even harder for such a futurist (who must denigrate the present to justify this dystopian vision) to accept that those methods are intensely user friendly and cost-effective. The methods include the internal organization of books and periodicals (tables of contents, chapter/article headings, running titles, page numbers, section headings, indexes, etc.), online catalogues and other bibliographic databases, periodical indexes and abstracts, classification schemes, subject heading lists, and the dedicated, disciplined work of cataloguers, bibliographers, and other creators of the interactive bibliographic structure. It is perfectly possible to walk into a major research library containing millions of volumes and locate a desired text or part of a text within minutes. This everyday occurrence may seem humdrum, but it is beyond the wildest dreams of any Mosaicist or Web-ster. The result of this activity, moreover, is access to a high-quality text or graphic that is secure in its provenance and instantly usable.

It is possible for us to preserve the best of what we have *and* to apply the techniques of bibliographic control (in which librarians are uniquely qualified) to the chaotic Net. Imagine a time in which one could use a well-organized real library *and* gain access to electronic resources that were as easy to locate, identify, and use as a well-ordered collection of books! I know that such a thing would disappoint those who have made a vocation of surfing the Net an alternative to living, but things are tough all over. After all, even California is not run to gratify the desires of ocean surfers. Let others ride the Third Wave of virtual libraries and virtual reality indefinitely; the rest of us have lives to lead, lives that will benefit from speedy and efficient access to recorded knowledge and information in all forms. It is the job of the real library of the future to continue well-established collections and services while applying organizational skills to clear the electronic wilderness for future seekers of knowledge and truth.

Why We Do Not Need an AACR3
What's in a Name?

Let me start by explaining that the name *"Anglo-American Cataloguing Rules,* Second Edition" is a misnomer. The name stemmed from the limited scope of the project as envisaged in the early 1970s—essentially to harmonize the British and North American texts of the 1967 AACR and to incorporate the ISBD(M) without changing the structure or principles of the rules. By the time it became evident that those modest aims had been transmuted by the forces of history and an entirely new code was aborning, it became politically necessary to preserve the pretense of continuity. Anyone who doubts that political decision need only look at the hysteria that gave rise to the War of AACR2 and imagine the response of the craven and reactionary had an entirely new name been rubbed in their faces! It would have been worth it to have endured a slightly longer storm and to have called the new code something like "English-language rules for cataloguing all library materials." The clumsily named AACR2R could have been a second edition of the ELRC and we could now be contemplating an ELRC3 without the fears and heightened expectations that must inevitably attend an "AACR3."

Why would a completely new name have been more truthful and desirable? Among other reasons, the 1967 AACR had much more in common with ALA 1949 (the "red book") and the *Rules for Descriptive Cataloging in the Library of Congress* (the "green book" of 1949) than it did with AACR2. In fact, whole chunks of the green book were incorporated into the North American text of AACR 1967. Taking the broad view, one can see three eras of English-language cataloguing codes. The first is that of the nineteenth-century single-author codes, those of Panizzi, Cutter, Jewett, and so on. The second is that of the twentieth-century pre-Lubetzky case-law codes drawn up by committees (this era ran from the Anglo-American rules of 1908 through the 1967 AACR). The third—that of the post-Lubetzky, post-ISBD codes—began with AACR2. Revisionist historians could allege that the 1967 code was, at least, the precursor to that era if not actually the first code in it, but that is not a supportable position when one takes into account that Lubetzky resigned (or was pushed?) from the editorship of the 1967 code precisely because it was not to be allowed to embody his ideas. Further, it should be noted that the descriptive chapters preceded the ISBDs and cannot, therefore, be said to be truly of the modern era.

Why AACR2 Represents True Change

When looked at objectively, it is clear that AACR2 represents a major change, comparable to that of Panizzi's rules and AA1908, because of the following.

AACR2 was the first code to integrate all media in both description *and* access points. As someone who was intimately involved with the development of both the ISBD(M) and the ISBD(G), I can state without fear of contradiction that the ISBD(M) was flawed in that it continued the "book-centric" descriptions of previous codes, whereas the later ISBD(G)—the basis of part I of AACR2—provided, for the first time, a comprehensive, media-neutral descriptive framework. As far as the rules on access points are concerned, part II of AACR2 is the first time that any cataloguing code considered names and titles on a medium-neutral basis. For example, names are based on the forms found in "chief sources of information," which are determined, medium by medium, with reference to the framework of ISBD.

AACR2 is the first cataloguing code that clearly delineates the distinction between *description* (of tangible objects, and now of defined electronic assemblages) and *access* (relating to works and not to manifestations of those works). I will admit that the language of AACR2 is not always clear and consistent when it comes to this distinction, but the principle is clear. If the explication of the principle is flawed, that is an editorial, not conceptual, failing and one relatively easily remedied. In this context, the placing of parts I and II of AACR2 is of symbolic importance. The cataloguer is led to proceed from the description of the physical object (or assemblage of electronic data) to the consideration of the work rather than the other way round.

Access points in AACR2 are based (not always entirely successfully) on the Lubetzkyan principled approach rather than the case-law method that had hobbled previous codes. It is true that political/strategic considerations again rear their ugly heads and that AACR2 contains some holdovers from the past. It is important to note, though, that those "case-law" holdovers are isolated in special rules that could easily be detached in a future revision (I will return to this point later).

AACR2 is consciously internationalist, though from the English-language point of view. That internationalism not only has made AACR2 the most widely used cataloguing code in history and the basis for a number of non–English-language codes, but it also has imposed the burden of remaining responsive to that global use. Proposals to change the *nature* of AACR2 should be greeted with considerable caution and a clear appraisal of the consequences of such change for libraries and catalogues throughout the world. This is the first code over which U.S. libraries have no veto power—something to be welcomed, not feared, in an era of globalization in bibliographic control as in so many other areas of life.

Though AACR2 preserved the main entry (yet more of the politics of bibliographic fear reinforced, in this instance, by the existence of the 1XX field in MARC), it showed the way toward the concept of authority records of equal value attached to descriptions and, thus, presages the ultimate elimination of this unnecessary complication of little relevance to the computerized catalogues of today. (On a point of personal privilege, I wish to state, with sorrow, that this is the only important area in which I have a view different from that of Seymour Lubetzky, the father of modern library cataloguing.)

AACR2 is the first code to embody the concept of one person having two or more bibliographic identities, that is, an "author" not necessarily being coexistent with a person. This is not a purely theoretical point. There is, for example, a book about the police novels of Ed McBain and, in framing the subject heading for that work, it is crucial to distinguish one bibliographic persona from others created by the same individual. This innovation is of considerable theoretical importance and represents one of the most radical breaks with past codes.

AACR2 provides an infinitely expandable framework (in both description and access) to accommodate new media and media yet unborn and has, hence, eliminated the need for "new" AACRs to deal with the problems such new media may pose.

The Context of AACR2

Some have said that a need exists for radical, structural change to AACR2. Others, myself included, believe that a need does exist for some change, but that the change should be gradual, evolutionary, and within the structures and principles of AACR2. If we are to evaluate the need for change and the nature of the change, it is imperative that we understand the real-world context of the cataloguing rules. That context is: the need for standardization because of cooperation and copy cataloguing; the emerging importance of the authority control concept as central to electronic bibliographic systems; other standards; and, in North America, the Library of Congress Rule Interpretations.

Most of these factors and influences are self-explanatory, but I would like to add a comment or two about "other standards" and the LCRIs. The other standards I am referring to are principally the ISBDs and MARC in its various manifestations. The former are our bridge to the cataloguers of the world; their significance in the context of the ideal of Universal Bibliographic Control cannot be underestimated. MARC is also of great international significance, for good and ill, and I have long given up on my youthful dreams of seeing MARC thoroughly overhauled to create a format fully in tune with current systems. Like Thomas Carlyle's acquaintance who said she accepted the Universe—to which he replied "By God, ma'am, you'd better!"—we must accept MARC, warts and all, but applaud all those who are seeking to modify its applications to conform to modern electronic bibliographic control systems. When it comes to LCRIs, we are as pious Catholics looking to the Church for guidance and our Vatican is LC. Like those religious folk, we complain when the word from on high is complicated or not to our liking. This is not LC's fault. They produce LCRIs because we ask them to, and I am sure they would be happy to get out of the interpretive business. In short, I have seen the enemy and he is us, and until cataloguing matures to the point when we can distinguish between necessary and foolish consistency, the LCRIs will be always with us.

What Do the AACR3 Folks Want?

I have read all the many statements from the American cataloguing community that call for change and, in effect if not always overtly, an AACR3. There seem to be four major areas of need and complaint. They are: "simplification," "flexibility," the perceived need for "strategic planning," and the creation of master records for "multiple versions."

"Simplification" is a very slippery word in the context of cataloguing. Do the people who ask for it want simpler rules? It can be argued that the wording of AACR2 is more direct and understandable than that of any previous code. Is the structure of AACR2 too complicated? It is true that

AACR2 is far more structured than previous codes, but that structure, once understood, is a benefit, not a barrier, to use. Are there too many rules? Here we may be on to something. There are too many rules for two distinct reasons. Various "special interests" insisted on loading up the rules with descriptive elaboration that is too detailed for the general cataloguer and not detailed enough for the specialist. The other reason for the superfluity of rules is that there are many hangovers from previous codes that were retained for political reasons (I will come to both topics later). Perhaps the true demand of the "simplifiers" is for minimal records without all that tedious authority control. That kind of simplification of cataloguing practice runs counter to the very notion of a code of cataloguing rules and should be resisted at all costs.

Flexibility is a basic attribute of AACR2. There has never been a code that was so accommodating to new cataloguing problems (because it is based on principle) and to new forms of communication (because of the ISBD(G) descriptive structure). Perhaps someone could explain the nature of the "flexibility" requested and reassure us all that it is not another code word for abandoning standards and good cataloguing practice.

Strategic planning as applied to cataloguing is one of the more bizarre notions currently being floated. It is clearly inapplicable to bibliographic standards and represents yet another example of the misappropriation of business management techniques and jargon and the attempt to apply them in areas to which they have no relevance. Strategic planning presupposes the need for change and is set up to create change. In this instance, it is yet another example of a solution in search of a problem.

Last, there has been some spectacularly misguided and misinformed discussion of the need to create "master records" for works that are manifested in many different physical forms. It is hard for me to believe that this notion has been put about by people who are cataloguers. Let me spell it out. Descriptions are of physical objects (and, nowadays, of defined assemblages of electronic data). It is literally impossible to have a single description of two or more different physical objects and/or electronic assemblages. Once the material has been described, the cataloguer looks at the manifestation in the light of the work (an intellectual construct that, by its nature, cannot be described) in order to assign access points (including uniform titles) and create authority files. This process, which should be understood by anyone who has taken Cataloguing I, clearly demonstrates that the idea of a "master record" for several manifestations of the same work is cataloguing nonsense.

If Not AACR3, What?

Some things could and should be done to improve AACR2 without changing its structure or principles.

1. We should get rid of all the "special" case-law rules (for example, the numerous special rules dealing with religious materials and laws).
2. We should prune descriptive rules of their over-elaboration in particular cases—those that are insufficient for the specialist cataloguer and too detailed for the general cataloguer (for example, in the rules for incunabula and maps). The needs of the specialist cataloguer and special collections could be catered to by specialist manuals created by the relevant cataloguing bodies and overseen and certified as true interpretations of AACR2 by the Joint Steering Committee.
3. We should resolve the issue of "unpublished" items (texts, video, sound, etc.) in a completely uniform manner across the chapters in part I.
4. We should develop new or revised chapters of part I to accommodate new media (especially electronic media, including those accessible only remotely).
5. We should study access issues for new media (especially electronic) with a view to seeing how the general rules hold up or need elaboration, without creating new case-law rules.
6. We should review part II with the authority record concept in mind (including addressing the main entry issue).
7. We should resolve the microform issue, not only by persuading LC to drop its "interpretation" that directly contradicts the letter and the spirit of the rule, but also by avoiding a similar debacle over the question of parallel print and electronic texts.
8. We should do a comprehensive review of the examples with a view to amending those that are no longer relevant and adding examples for new media.
9. We should create a consolidation of the unified MARC format and AACR2 and bear in mind the possibility of a principle-based subject term code to be added to create a complete cataloguer's resource.
10. We should ask LC to review and curtail the LCRI program (for example, have them cease issuing rule interpretations not concerned with important questions of access).

AACR2 represents not just a major achievement in the Anglo-American cataloguing tradition, but also a beacon of a new age of global cataloguing. We should celebrate and consolidate what we have wrought and work toward making an ever-improving AACR2 the basis for international cooperation devoted to attaining Universal Bibliographic Control.

Note

1. Frederick G. Kilgour, "Effectiveness of Surname-Title-Words Searches by Scholars," *Journal of the American Society for Information Science* 46 (March 1995): 145–51.

# AACR and Authority Control

Barbara B. Tillett

Libraries invest a great deal of time and money in organizing the materials we select in order to assure that they are easily available for use. Particularly in the United States, we have recognized the benefits of sharing the work of cataloging in order to reduce costs. We have agreed to standardize our cataloging practices to facilitate sharing of bibliographic and authority records so we aren't all redundantly doing the same work. Over the years we have grown more and more alike in cataloging, in great part through accepting a standard set of cataloging rules and rule interpretations and, more recently, through sharing the same resource authority file to enable consistency in our forms of authorized headings.

Objectives of the Catalog

In the past we have found it convenient to establish single authorized forms for headings following cataloging rules. The single form assures collocation, and the provision of references facilitates finding. The finding and collocation functions of the catalog derive from Cutter's objects of a catalog and reflect basic assumptions about why we create catalogs instead of mere finding lists. We control the forms of names, titles, and subjects in our catalogs to enable our users to confidently retrieve all bibliographic records without having to request all synonyms or variant forms of name or title. We control forms of names, titles, and subjects to enable our users to confidently retrieve precisely those bibliographic records that are appropriate without also retrieving homonyms or non-unique titles or names. We control the forms of names, titles, and subjects in our catalogs to facilitate directing users to related works.

This use of an established or authorized single form is not really necessary in a computer-based catalog. As early as 1969, Seymour Lubetzky examined the rule prescribing that an author be identified in the catalog by the name by which he or she is most commonly identified in his or her works, with references from the other names used by the author. As Lubetzky noted, this relates to Cutter's objective for a catalog to show what works the library has by a particular author. He noted that this objective could be

> accomplished more easily and simply by identifying the different names and pseudonyms used by an author as designating the same author and devising a program by means of which an inquiry for the works of an author by any one of his names will produce a listing of all his works published under the different names. The gain achieved in this way would be a material simplification of the process of cataloging resulting from elimination of the problem of choice of name by which an author is to be identified in the catalog.[1]

Some early computer systems were designed with a literal approach to this suggestion of displaying all bibliographic entries associated with all forms of name when the user asked for one form, but such systems proved to be confusing when users found unexpected names in response to their queries (pseudonyms they didn't realize were the same person, etc.). Later systems informed users that the name they selected was associated with other names for that person used in the catalog, and users were given the ability to continue with just a single form or any or all of the variations. The point is that a single form of name is unnecessary for collocation, if we can link the various forms and display them together.

We may still want a rule for selecting a "default" form to use in alphabetical displays of retrieved records. Such a rule would open up the sharing of access control records to an international audience.

AACR and Authority Control

The Anglo-American Cataloguing Rules, second edition, part II, deals with choice of access points for main and added entries, with the form of headings used as access points, and with references. However, in the beginning of AACR2, Rule 0.5 includes instructions about making "main entries" in the sense of a "bibliographic record," and then refers to alternative "headings" or "added entries" in the sense of alternative "access points." It would be clearer to distinguish between the creation of a record for bibliographic description and the identification of access points to be used to organize the record in or retrieve it from a set of records.

AACR2 does mention bibliographic records and vaguely mentions "records" for references. Rule 26.0 instructs the cataloger to record "every reference under the name heading or uniform title to which it refers in order to make possible the correction or deletion of the reference."[2] How to do so is not addressed.

There are separate MARC formats for bibliographic and authority records, although the bibliographic format allows one to record references in bibliographic records. However, recording references in bibliographic records leads to having to make those references redundantly each time another heading is encountered with variant forms. This entry of variant forms in bibliographic records is still being followed by the National Library of Canada. In the United States, we have preferred instead to record such variations once only in an authority record. This saves the cataloger's time and still controls access through references, if we continue to prefer a single authorized form of name.

Online we can use the variant forms traditionally called references to get to bibliographic records directly, if we set up our systems to do so. However, many systems typically include an interim step to explain the "authorized" form. We could let the user choose the authorized form or let the library do so, but for now we are hanging on to card-based models when we could be moving on to other means of controlled access.

Technologies Driving the Devices We Use

In book catalogs, full bibliographic information was provided once in the bibliographic entry. The user was directed to that entry from a variety of access points, such as names of authors, variant titles, subjects, and so on, through references to the entry. We had entries and references. Entries were grouped to collocate by the principle of primary authorship under the first author for works, and works were collocated under the author's name using standardized forms of titles (when there were many manifestations).

In card catalogs, the full bibliographic entry was carried on a card that could be reproduced and have headings typed at the top of it. The cards could be filed in an alphabetical arrangement that enabled us to have groupings to collocate all the records for works in multiple places in the catalog under all access points. Main entries and added entries could be interfiled, some catalogs choosing to subgroup the filing order to place main entries first and secondary entries following. Just as in book catalogs, we continued to create references, but now on cards that instructed the user to "see" or "see also" other headings. Rather than being used for added access, references came to be used instead for directing the user from variant forms to the authorized form or between two authorized forms that were related in some way. We used tracings on bibliographic records to keep track of added entries we had made so that we could easily locate them when needed for maintenance or withdrawals.

Some libraries created card files of authority cards, known as authority files. The purpose of authority cards or authority records was to:

document decisions about authorized forms,
document cross-references made, and
record sources checked in either establishing the authorized
    form or discovering the variant forms used as references.

Authority cards were seen as a housekeeping tool to direct the creation of reference cards to be filed into the card catalog and to facilitate maintenance of the catalog by identifying reference cards made so they could be retrieved easily when needed for corrections or removal.

With online catalogs, we continued to emulate card catalogs, providing bibliographic entries (now called bibliographic records). We now had no need to prepare separate added entries but instead could use tracings as access points for retrieving bibliographic records. We continued the use of a main entry heading in order to organize alphabetical displays that preserve the principle of authorship, acknowledging primary responsibility for intellectual or artistic content when such responsibility exists. Thus, in a display or arrangement of bibliographic entries under a given access point, such as under a subject heading, we can subarrange the entries in an order we feel will be most useful to our users, collocating the works of an author. We also use the main entry heading as the initial element in bibliographic citations, so we can cite works as the object of a relationship. (This citation function was recognized in AACR2 Rule 0.5 as being one reason for retaining the concept of main entry.)

In addition to the traditional collocations of entries by author, title, and subject in card and book catalogs, computer-based catalogs allow us many more ways to display retrieved records, gathering them together by such things as date or country of publication, by language, or by combinations of access: subject and language, and so on. Some of these access points are controlled and some are uncontrolled. It would be useful in the next cataloging rules to identify which information should be controlled and why.

We control subject access because of the rich variety of synonyms that can be used for topics and because we want users to get to the group of records on a given subject as easily as possible. Our descriptive cataloging rules suggest that we control names (personal, corporate, conference, geographic) and titles (including author/title combinations). However, control of titles is still ambiguous. There is still a mix of using added entries for title variations and using references in authority records for variant titles of works. Using control records for title variations would facilitate online retrieval of manifestations of works.

Uniform Titles

A discussion of authority control for titles requires first a look at why we have uniform titles. With AACR2 the term "uniform title" is used for an unfortunate mix of a variety of standardized titles. In earlier rules and filing instructions, conventional titles, standardized titles, form headings, filing titles, and unique or distinctive titles were differentiated. AACR2 mixes these up, as if they were the same. They are not.

Although chapter 25 for uniform titles is optional, uniform titles can be useful for providing a controlled name for a work, for organizing large files, and when citing a related work. When we have very large files and many bibliographic records for the same bibliographic entity, it is convenient to group them together using a uniform title for collocation, subarranging by date or whatever attribute is useful. This can be done easily in an online catalog, if we provide a collocating uniform title (often author/title combination). In current rules, we use a title in the original language by which a work has become best known (Rule 25.3).

We may also find it useful to create form headings when trying to collocate musical works under a prolific composer or legal works under a jurisdiction. It is the main entry heading/title combination that is useful for collocation and retrieval, but some online catalogs index the title portion alone for title retrieval, which can cause much confusion because that is not its intended use. "Selections" alone is not a helpful title on which to retrieve unless you have further subarranging devices.

Without guidance in the cataloging rules as to why we are providing this access and what portions of it should be controlled, online catalog designers went off on their own with a literal approach to grouping uniform titles separately from titles proper, since they were tagged separately. Current rules do not allow for adding a uniform title when it is the same as the title proper, an economical decision in card catalogs. However, computers often are programmed to be too literal and arrange such entries separately. Ideally we would have sophisticated matching algorithms and computer interfiling of such titles.

We also have uniform titles that are really distinctive titles, particularly for serials where it is important to differentiate between similar titles. The point here is not collocation but, rather, separation in order to uniquely identify different serials. The rules should let us know why we need such distinctions and suggest ways to make them.

Conceptual Models and Controlled Access

In the past 15 years, several attempts have been made to describe conceptual models of the bibliographic universe, including models developed by the National Library of Canada and the Library of Congress and, most recently, by the IFLA Study Group on Functional Requirements for Bibliographic Records. These models have in common the following concepts:

bibliographic entities (e.g., works, manifestations, items, copies);
bibliographic relationships (e.g., equivalent, derivative, referential, companion, additive, whole/part, coincidental); and
bibliographic attributes (title, statement of responsibility, publisher, date of publication, etc.).

Entities for controlled access are also an essential component of many of these models. We may see bibliographic and authority information packaged differently in the future so that description and access are separate but linked. One such model was presented in the late 1970s by Michael Gorman, and I later presented variations of it at a LITA conference and at the Airlie House Conference on Multiple Versions. The most simplified structure of that model includes descriptive records, holdings records, and control records (see Figure 1). Descriptive records contain information transcribed from the item being cataloged or may be derived from an electronic text directly, augmented with notes and subject information. Selected descriptive/subject information would be marked for those portions that should be controlled for access, and a link would be made to the corresponding access control records. The descriptive/subject

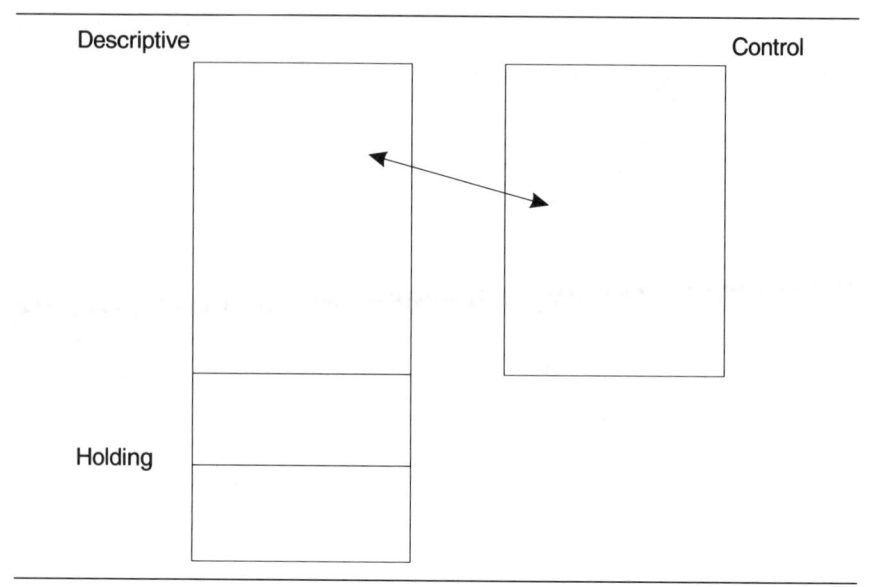

[Figure: Two vertical rectangles labeled "Descriptive" (left) and "Control" (right) with a double-headed arrow between them; the left rectangle has a lower section labeled "Holding".]

Figure 1. Record structure

records could be in multiple hierarchies of subordinate bibliographic records for various equivalent manifestations or for linking multiple versions and those in turn could be linked to specific item- or piece-level records for the holdings of a given library (to include such information as shelf number, location, special notes about restricted use, etc.).

Such a structure reflects a clear distinction between description and access, a concept that unfortunately is becoming more and more blurred and confused in attempts to reduce redundancy in the MARC formats.

Resource Authority Files—Internationalization

As automation moves ahead, we will develop systems for machine-assisted checking, verification, and validation of information catalogers feel is useful for access. Machine-generated base access control records will become routine and will feed into international resource bibliographic and access control files. These international resource files may be real or virtual, depending on which is most cost-effective for record creation, distribution, and maintenance.

The Library of Congress establishes about 100,000 new name authority records each year, about 10,000 new series authority records, and about 9,000 new subject terms. These figures are expected to increase with the assistance of cooperative partners contributing to the shared resource authority files.

Work is underway to expand contributions to our shared resource authority files and bibliographic files through the Program for Cooperative Cataloging. This cooperative work has been going on for several years under the aegis of such programs as the National Coordinated Cataloging Program and the Name Authority Cooperative Project. Recently the British Library has been working with the National Library of Canada and the Library of Congress to develop an Anglo-American Authority File. Work has already begun to bring together cataloging practices and MARC formats, a giant step toward increased sharing of the work of cataloging.

In looking at internationalization of authority work, we must not forget the substantial work conducted over the years under the auspices of IFLA to enable Universal Bibliographic Control. Tom Delsey's article, "Authority Control in an International Context," is a particularly good summary of this work.[3]

Delsey reminds us that beginning with the 1961 Paris Principles, IFLA sought to provide guidelines and basic agreements at the international level to facilitate shared cataloging. In 1980, IFLA issued *Form and Structure of Corporate Headings,* on the heels of its *Names of Persons* (1977; new edition, 1995). Both of these publications recognized and respected the national traditions of language, culture, and social structure that obtain in cataloging conventions.

The IFLA guidelines prefer the vernacular as the basis for authoritative headings. The dilemma, of course, lies in trying to respect the country of origin's preferences while meeting the needs of one's own users. Especially problematic are geographic names used in headings for governments; titles, epithets, and qualifiers for personal and corporate names; and headings for legal documents and officials of state.

The first principle of Universal Bibliographic Control is that each nation assumes responsibility for establishing authoritative headings for its national authors. The second principle of UBC is that all other countries are expected to accept such headings as being authoritative. They are to forgo their own national conventions and their own users' conventions in order to facilitate exchange of authority records at the international level. Understandably, this has been difficult.

Today, the name *is* the entity; that is, we equate the name for an entity with the entity itself. The dilemma is that there is apt to be much more agreement on what an entity is and what its characteristics are than on what single form of its name everybody in the world should use. We need to move away from this mind-set to recognize that an entity may have many names and leave the choice of which is considered "correct" or preferred to the user or individual library. I suggest that international authority records could instead become access control records, wherein we could record the preferred form as established by each country, or we could link access control records for separate languages requiring variant reference structures.

In 1978, IFLA conducted a study on authority files and established the Working Group on an International Authority System that standardized the content and structure of authority records in print and machine-readable form and proposed a "system" for authority control and exchange of authority data on an international scale. They proposed a network of interrelated national databases of authority records with a central facility to control the system—that is, to manage links between related authority records from various national centers and to direct packages of authority data to appropriate national centers.

The Working Group envisioned a standard number for an authority entry—the ISAN, International Standard Authority Number, like the ISBN and ISSN—to be present in all variant authority records and in bibliographic records after being registered through UBC. Any subsequent bibliographic or authority records submitted to the international resource files would trigger automatic adjustment of the form to what was required at the national level. However, IFLA ran into problems in administering such a system to assign numbers.

The Anglo-American Authority File approach is to have a governing body consisting of the British Library, the National Library of Canada, and the Library of Congress, building on the resource file at the Library of Congress. The AAAF concept is similar to the IFLA vision in that each country would be responsible for headings within the purview of its national origins and would accept headings submitted by the others. We at LC hope that the resource authority file will be used worldwide, and we will continue to accept contributions from all participants in our cooperative programs.

Future Rules

What should we ask for in our future rules for authority control?

1. The rules should guide us in the creation of access control records. They should include clear guidelines on what information in a bibliographic record should be linked to access control records.

2. The rules should include suggested structures for standard forms of names and titles, at the very least to provide a default when users have no preferred form they wish to use. The rules should include guidance for which variations to use once computer normalization and matching algorithms gain sophistication. They could even remind us of what system capabilities to provide, such as enabling retrieval from portions of compound names, even if we need no longer to explicitly enter such variations as references.
3. The rules should continue to provide guidance on choice of entry (which we may call citation form), to ensure that we can link related works through citation.
4. The rules should provide guidance, as earlier rules did, on the principles we should observe in the arrangement of bibliographic records, especially the subarrangement of entries.

We have not come as far toward computer-assisted authority control as I had hoped when I conducted a survey of authority control in 1984, and our automated systems have made very slow progress. This, however, is the area where the biggest payoff is to be expected for increased productivity (both for the cataloger and for the user), and we must persist in our attempts to ensure that this basic activity is performed in a cost-effective manner.

Authority control in the twenty-first century will mean controlled access through links between bibliographic description and access control records. We will gradually move away from the structure of records that currently confines us (i.e., the MARC format) to future system architectures and capabilities designed to manage bibliographic information. Despite our very slow start, I hope that our momentum will enable faster development of systems that incorporate the conceptual models described earlier and, hence, improved systems for our library staff and users.

Notes

1. Seymour Lubetzky, *Principles of Cataloging* (Los Angeles, Calif.: Institute of Library Research, University of California, 1969), 94.
2. *Anglo-American Cataloguing Rules,* 2d ed. (Chicago: American Library Association, 1978), 540.
3. Tom Delsey, "Authority Control in an International Context," in *Authority Control in the Online Environment: Considerations and Practices,* Barbara B. Tillett, ed. (New York: Haworth Press, 1989), 13–28.

Editions: Brainstorming for AACR2000

Martha M. Yee

We all of us, grave or light, get our thoughts tangled in metaphors, and act fatally on the strength of them.
—George Eliot, *Middlemarch*

Things should be made as simple as possible, but no simpler.
—Alfred Einstein

In an attempt to divine the cataloging future with regard to editions, I will first establish some rough definitions. Then I will try to outline the goals and objectives to be met in describing and providing access to editions. Finally, I will ask how we can best meet those goals and objectives.

Please note that I have put the term *brainstorming* into my title in order to emphasize that the following is an essay about what the *ideal* approach might be for creating a national catalog built by cooperative cataloging. I have ignored all the political and economic obstacles that would lie in the path to creating such a catalog, if it were ever decided to do so. In other words, I have taken *brainstorming* to mean that one can temporarily shed one's obligation to be practical and dream a little.

I had a great deal of help on this chapter from John Attig, Jo Crawford, Sara Shatford Layne, and Brian Schottlaender, and would like to thank them for taking time from their busy schedules to catch my errors, argue with me, and suggest ways to strengthen my arguments.—*The Author*

Before beginning, perhaps I ought to discuss which parts of AACR2 might be affected by changes discussed here. In the narrowest approach to change, only the glossary definition of the term *edition* might need tinkering with. In the broadest approach, the entire code could be affected, since one of the main purposes of the descriptive part of a cataloging record is to identify a particular edition of a particular work and distinguish it from other editions of that work. Each element of the description has a role to play in that identification and distinction process. The overall organization of chapters 1 through 12 of AACR2 undoubtedly needs work, now that any format can be combined with any other(s). In addition, one of the main purposes of headings, uniform titles, and references (chapters 21 through 26) is to demonstrate relationships among the various editions of a work. How much of the code needs change depends on the degree to which the creation, distribution, access, and use of the documents we are trying to describe have changed and will continue to change as we undergo a tremendous technological revolution.

Some Definitions

To begin, in order to provide some quick context for the discussion that follows, I am going to define the following terms by way of example, rather than trying to develop full explanations, complete with reasoned and watertight arguments for defining these concepts this way. (Those interested in fuller explanations I refer to my series of articles on "work," published in *Cataloging & Classification Quarterly*,[1] as well as my series of articles on "manifestations" and "near-equivalents," published in *Library Resources & Technical Services*.[2])

Work:	Shakespeare's *Macbeth*
Version:[3]	A translation of *Macbeth* into German
Edition:	A second edition with corrections of the translation of *Macbeth* into German
Near-equivalent:	A microform copy of the second edition with corrections of the translation of *Macbeth* into German
Copies:	Two copies of the microform near-equivalent of the second edition with corrections of the translation of *Macbeth* into German

I should mention one other concept here, that of "super-work." Some works spin off into other works: They are made into operas, plays, movies, and so on. When that happens, some would argue that the original work becomes a "super-work" with other works derived from it. Two examples of works derived from a super-work would be the films that Roman Polanski and Akira Kurosawa made of *Macbeth, Polanski's Macbeth* and *Throne of Blood,* respectively. Most would recognize that these films are not simply editions of *Macbeth,* but are new works. However, they certainly have been derived from Shakespeare's play and should be brought to the attention of users interested in performances of *Macbeth.*

In this chapter, I want to focus on the concept of "edition."[4] I would like to propose the following working definition for the term *edition:* an item that is essentially the same work as another item, but with some differences significant to users. The first *LRTS* article mentioned earlier contains an extensive discussion of the types of differences that can occur and of the significance (or lack thereof) of these differences to users. Following are brief lists of the major types of differences, classified into two categories: (1) significant differences that might need a separate record to express them adequately to users, and (2) less-significant differences that can perhaps be recorded on subrecords. This classification, of course, is my own, and does not, unfortunately in my opinion, correspond to current practice. I jump right into it here in order to stimulate thought and discussion on potential directions our cataloging rules could take.

Notice that the focus in these lists is on differences that are observable by a working cataloger. One of the questions I attempted to address in my dissertation research on moving-image materials was that of how often differences occur that are *not* observable by working catalogers. This question could profitably be posed for other types of materials as well, and the answers could bear on future approaches to the problem in the cataloging rules.

1. Significant differences that might need a separate record to express them:
   a. Change in title;
   b. Change in series title;
   c. Change in statement of responsibility, including subsidiary responsibility, signaling change in actual intellectual and artistic content (commentators, editors, translators, illustrators, etc.);
   d. Explicit statement of change in intellectual and artistic content (e.g., revised edition, enlargements, abridgments);
   e. Change in extent (i.e., change in actual intellectual and artistic content, or potential change because of, for example, resetting of type);

f. Explicit change in list of contents (e.g., different songs or different takes of songs listed on CD compared with sound recording disc or audiocassette); and

g. Change in language.

2. Less-significant differences that can perhaps be recorded on subrecords:
   a. Change in edition statement without corresponding change in intellectual and artistic content (e.g., paperback edition);
   b. Change in distributor or distribution date or both without corresponding change in intellectual and artistic content; and
   c. Change in physical format without corresponding change in intellectual or artistic content (e.g., a microform copy of a text, or an audiocassette copy of a CD; this category is commonly known as a reproduction).

The Future

If every document is likely to become an electronic document in the future, one has to wonder if some of these types of differences might change. For example, if pathways to documents become relatively stable eventually, and invisible to most users, will the publication/distribution area of the cataloging record tend to wither away? Or does this area have other functions besides that of recording where one can obtain a copy? If so, will such other functions continue to operate? For example, some might argue that publication source can bestow prestige on a document (or conversely, cast suspicion on it). On the other hand, perhaps that is a type of responsibility that could be recorded with other statements of responsibility.

In the current state of electronic publication, the pathways to documents are far from stable; in addition, the same document can be available from a number of different sources and, therefore, have a number of different URLs. Different documents in different locations can have significant intellectual and artistic differences over time as one is revised but another is not. In fact, some types of electronic publications can be put up so differently in two different sites, with such different types of access to the document available, that it could be argued that each time the document is put up a new edition is created. Ownership—even authorship—of documents seems to be in a state of flux, leading one to wonder if we are headed for the kind of community ownership of a text that used to prevail in oral cultures. In this context, as John Attig points out, publication information may be an indication of authenticity of a version that has some provenance relationship to the original creator of the document. If these trends continue, they will have the effect of increasing the importance of the "distributor/publisher" (i.e., the place at which the document can be accessed), rather than diminishing it, and will simply exacerbate the current problems with editions and near-equivalents.

If all formats eventually can be run on any computer system, will parts of the physical description area of the cataloging record, as well as its early warning flag, the GMD, tend to wither away? Without the need to be so concerned about whether particular playback equipment will be available, will there be a tendency to generalize the physical description more, so as merely to indicate the presence or predominance of image (moving or still), sound, or text? What function will the physical description serve?

Certainly, at the current time it is not yet possible to run even all-text formats on any given computer system, thus the current proliferation of such near-equivalents as the document in ASCII, Acrobat or PostScript format, and so on.

One can't imagine the extent statement losing its usefulness, can one? How will extent be communicated for electronic documents, when we no longer have physical volumes and pages? If character counts (for textual materials), frame counts (for visual materials), and playing time (for sound and moving-image visual materials) were to become the norm, it might become much easier to use extent to spot actual change in intellectual and artistic content. We could even envision computer programs that carry out comparisons between two items and highlight differences for catalogers to summarize for users, and for users to display on demand.

Goals and Objectives

What would we like our catalogs to do for us and for our users with regard to editions? In the past, we have had two sets of answers for this question. One set of answers is found in the objectives of descriptive cataloging, which were actually included in AACR1, but have been dropped from AACR2. "Descriptive cataloging" here refers only to the preparation of the body of the record, as opposed to choice and form of access points. According to AACR1, the objectives of descriptive cataloging are:

> 1) to state the significant features of an item with the purpose of distinguishing it from other items and describing its scope, contents, and bibliographic relation to other items

2) to present these data in an entry which can be integrated with the entries for other items in the catalog, and which will respond best to the interests of most users of the catalog. . . . Extent of description: The item is described as fully as necessary to achieve the objectives stated above, but with economy of data and expression.[5]

In other words, we would like the description to *distinguish* this edition from other editions of the same work. We would also like the description to *identify* it as being the same work as other editions of the work it represents. And finally, we would like the distinction and identification to be carried out as efficiently as possible, "with economy of data and expression."

The other set of answers is found in the "objects," or functions of the catalog, first recorded by Cutter, further developed by Lubetzky, and adopted as an international standard at the International Conference on Cataloguing Principles in Paris in 1961:

2. Functions of the catalogue
   The catalogue should be an efficient instrument for ascertaining
   2.1 whether the library contains a particular book specified by
      (a) its author and title, *or*
      (b) if the author is not named in the book, its title alone, *or*
      (c) if the author and title are inappropriate or insufficient for identification, a suitable substitute for the title; and
   2.2 (a) which works by a particular author and
      (b) which editions of a particular work are in the library.[6]

Function 2.2b is that of being an efficient instrument for ascertaining which editions of a particular work are in the library. In other words, we would like our catalogs to enable users to see all the editions of a particular work so that those users can make up their own minds about which edition might best meet their needs.[7] To do this, we need some sort of linking mechanism to tie together all the editions of a work in a particular catalog.

Lest we think of abandoning that goal (the linking goal, which is admittedly a very difficult one to carry out), Ross Atkinson reminds us, in his recent article, that linking—or what he refers to as "reference to the citation"—is the fundamental goal of all libraries and of the humanities in general.[8] To paraphrase his arguments (I hope he will forgive me), humanists ask the question, "How did we get here (the present) from there (the past)?" In contrast, scientists are more apt to ask, "How can we get there (the future) from here (the present)?" Our job as librarians is to keep and organize for access the cultural record of our society, so that (1) humanists can try to answer their question, and (2) new scientists can be trained based on how scientists of the past have done their work. It is essential for the user who is searching the cultural record to see demonstrated the relationships among the works of an author and among the editions of a work, as called for by the functions of the catalog, because editions of a work are the primary source material for studying the history of the work. The works of greatest cultural and historical importance are generally the ones that go into multiple editions.

How Can We Best Identify and Distinguish Editions?

Current practice is to create a separate cataloging record for each edition and near-equivalent. (This practice is not contained in AACR2 itself, but rather in Library of Congress Rule Interpretations and guidelines issued by the bibliographic utilities). Because of this practice regarding near-equivalents, our national databases are cluttered with hundreds of records that undoubtedly represent the same edition of the same work, with differences only in physical format, distributor, or distribution date. The user often must read through whole screens of data to find the minute differences between these items (see Figures 1 through 8). This practice certainly could not be described as meeting the objective of identifying and distinguishing using "economy of data and expression."

The *Guidelines for the Description of Reproductions* developed by the ALA Committee on Cataloging: Description and Access have attempted to devise a hierarchically organized description for one type of near-equivalent, the reproduction; however, they have not been widely implemented so far.[9] In the process of devising the guidelines, the possibility of using the USMARC holdings format to create subrecords for reproductions was considered and rejected, because it would be so difficult for the existing national databases to accommodate this approach due to logical problems with conflating holdings information (which library holds what volumes of what titles) with near-equivalent information. For clear displays, such information needs to be kept distinct. (See my article "Manifestations and Near-Equivalents" for a more extended discussion of this problem.)

What might the future hold in the way of a solution to this problem? As I have attempted to argue here, the problem is actually much bigger than just that of reproductions, although the speed with which records for reproductions are cluttering up our national databases makes that part of the problem particularly vivid for most of us. The real problem lies with our inability to effectively and consistently share identified bibliographic relationships as part of our shared cataloging programs.[10]

Editions: Brainstorming for AACR2000 47

```
        OCLC:   176917              Rec stat:   n
        Entered:        19711201    Replaced:   19931223    Used:       19970527
►  Type:   a        ELvl:   I       Srce:   d   Audn:       Ctrl:       Lang:   eng
   BLvl:   m        Form:           Conf:   0   Biog:       MRec:       Ctry:   xx
                    Cont:           GPub:       Fict:   0   Indx:   0
        Desc:       Ills:           Fest:   0   DtSt:   s   Dates:  1902,   ¶
►   1   010         02-29255 ¶
►   2   040         CDC ǂc CDC ǂd WSU ¶
►   3   019         359306 ¶
►   4   050 0       PZ3.S6665 ǂb H31 ǂa PR3694 ¶
►   5   082         823/.6 ¶
►   6   090         ǂb ¶
►   7   049         CLUM
►   8   100 1       Smollett, Tobias George, ǂd 1721-1771. ¶
►   9   245 14      The expedition of Humphry Clinker ¶
►  10   260         New York, ǂb Century, ǂc 1902. ¶
►  11   300         372 p. ǂb front. ¶
►  12   490 0       The English comedie humaine ¶
►  13   500         Cover title: Humphry Clinker. ¶
►  14   740 01      Humphry Clinker. ¶
```

Figure 1. An edition of *The Expedition of Humphry Clinker* published by Century in 1902

```
        OCLC:   9292587             Rec stat:   n
        Entered:        19830309    Replaced:   19940307    Used:       19960308
►  Type:   a        ELvl:   I       Srce:   d   Audn:       Ctrl:       Lang:   eng
   BLvl:   m        Form:           Conf:   0   Biog:       MRec:       Ctry:   nyu
                    Cont:           GPub:       Fict:   0   Indx:   0
        Desc:   a   Ills:           Fest:   0   DtSt:   s   Dates:  1906,   ¶
►   1   040         FDU ǂc FDU ¶
►   2   090         PR3694 ǂb .E8 1906 ¶
►   3   090         ǂb ¶
►   4   049         CLUM ¶
►   5   100 1       Smollett, Tobias George, ǂd 1721-1771. ¶
►   6   245 14      The expedition of Humphry Clinker / ǂc Tobias George Smollett. ¶
►   7   260         New York : ǂb Century, ǂc 1906, c1902. ¶
►   8   300         372 p. : ǂb front. ; ǂc 21 cm. ¶
►   9   490 0       The English comedie humaine ¶
►  10   500         Cover title: Humphry Clinker. ¶
►  11   740 01      Humphry Clinker. ¶
```

Figure 2. An edition of *The Expedition of Humphry Clinker* published by Century in 1906. Note that the paging (372 p.) is the same; it is therefore undoubtedly the same edition (in the sense of a setting of type).

```
     OCLC:   4599336            Rec stat:    c
     Entered:        19790130   Replaced:    19950223       Used:       19970520
 ▶   Type:   g       ELvl:   I  Srce:   d    Audn:   g      Ctrl:       Lang:    eng
     BLvl:   m       TMat:   v  GPub:        AccM:          MRec:       Ctry:    miu
     Desc:   i       Time:   171        Tech:   1    DtSt:   r     Dates:  1978,1969 ¶
 ▶    1   040        GZR ǂc GZR ǂd OCL ¶
 ▶    2   007        v ǂb f ǂd c ǂe b ǂf a ǂg h ǂh o ¶
 ▶    3   019        4599427 ¶
 ▶    4   045        x4x4 ¶
 ▶    5   090        ǂb ¶
 ▶    6   049        CLUM ¶
 ▶    7   245  00    Patton ǂh [Videorecording] / ǂc Twentieth Century-Fox Film
 Corp. ¶
 ▶    8   260        Farmington Hills, Mich. : ǂb Magnetic Video Corp., ǂc 1978,
 [made 1969] ¶
 ▶    9   300        2 cassettes, 171 min. : ǂb sd., col. ; ǂc 1/2 in. ¶
 ▶   10   500        VHS. ¶
 ▶   11   500        A videocassette release of the motion picture. ¶
 ▶   12   500        Based on factual material from the books Patton: ordeal and
 triumph, by Ladislas Farago, and A soldier's story, by Omar N. Bradley. ¶
 ▶   13   511        George C. Scott, Karl Malden. ¶
 ▶   14   508        Producer, Frank McCarthy; director, Franklin J. Schaffner;
 screenplay, Francis Ford Coppola, Edmund H. North; music, Jerry Goldsmith. ¶
 ▶   15   520        Adventure drama of World War II American general George S.
 Patton. ¶
 ▶   16   600  10    Patton, George S. ǂq (George Smith), ǂd 1885-1945 ǂx Drama. ¶
 ▶   17   700  1     Farago, Ladislas. ǂt Patton: ordeal and triumph. ¶
 ▶   18   700  1     Bradley, Omar Nelson, ǂd 1893-1981. ǂt A soldier's story. ¶
 ▶   19   710  2     Twentieth Century-Fox Film Corporation. ¶
```

Figure 3. A VHS videocassette of *Patton* released in 1978 by Magnetic Video Corp.

```
OCLC:    14115305              Rec stat:    c
Entered:          19860820     Replaced:    19950412      Used:     19970318
▶ Type:  g          ELvl:   I    Srce:   d    Audn:        Ctrl:          Lang:    eng
  BLvl:  m          TMat:   v    GPub:        AccM:        MRec:          Ctry:    miu
  Desc:  a          Time:   171  Tech:   1    DtSt:   s    Dates: 1984,       ¶
▶  1   040       IEZ ǂc IEZ ǂd OCL ¶
▶  2   090       ǂb ¶
▶  3   049       CLUM ¶
▶  4   245  00   Patton ǂh videorecording. ¶
▶  5   260       Farmington Hills, MI : ǂb CBS/Fox Video, ǂc 1969, 1984. ¶
▶  6   300       2 videocassettes (171 min.) : ǂb sd., col. ; ǂc 1/2 in. ¶
▶  7   500       Videocassette release of 1969 motion picture by Twentieth
Century-Fox Film Corporation. ¶
▶  8   511  1    George C. Scott, Karl Malden. ¶
▶  9   508       Screeplay by Francis Ford Coppola, Edmund H. North; producer,
Frank McCarthy; director, Franklin J. Schaffner. ¶
▶ 10   520       The World War II adventures of the controversial American
general, George S. Patton. ¶
▶ 11   500       VHS format. ¶
▶ 12   500       "1005" ¶
▶ 13   500       Hi-Fi stereo. ¶
▶ 14   600  10   Patton, George S. ǂq (George Smith), ǂd 1885-1945. ¶
▶ 15   700  1    Schaffner, Franklin J. ¶
▶ 16   700  1    Scott, George C., ǂd 1927- ¶
▶ 17   700  1    Malden, Karl. ¶
▶ 18   710  2    CBS Fox Video. ¶
```

Figure 4. A VHS videocassette of *Patton* released in 1984 by CBS/Fox Video. Playing time is still 171 min., so it is probably identical to the previous one.

```
OCLC:    28896284              Rec stat:      n
Entered:     19930927          Replaced:      19930927        Used:          19930927
▶ Type:   a          ELvl:  I       Srce:  d      Audn:           Ctrl:          Lang:  eng
  BLvl:   m          Form:           Conf:  0     Biog:           MRec:          Ctry:  xx
                     Cont:  b        GPub:         Fict:  0       Indx:  0
  Desc:   a          Ills:           Fest:  0     DtSt:  s        Dates: 1993,      ¶
▶  1   040        CLU ǂc CLU ¶
▶  2   090        LD791.9.L5 ǂb Y35 ¶
▶  3   090        ǂb ¶
▶  4   049        CLUM ¶
▶  5   100 1      Yee, Martha M. ¶
▶  6   245 10     Moving image works and manifestations / ǂc by Martha Mikkelson
Yee. ¶
▶  7   260        ǂc 1993. ¶
▶  8   300        xii, 230 leaves ; ǂc 28 cm. ¶
▶  9   502        Thesis (Ph. D.)--UCLA, 1993. ¶
▶ 10   500        Vita. ¶
▶ 11   504        Bibliography: leaves 203-230. ¶
▶ 12   650 0      Cataloging of motion pictures. ¶
```

Figure 5. Thesis—the original, cataloged at UCLA

```
OCLC:    29644339              Rec stat:      n
Entered:     19940118          Replaced:      19940118        Used:          19950131
▶ Type:   a          ELvl:  I       Srce:  d      Audn:           Ctrl:          Lang:  eng
  BLvl:   m          Form:  r        Conf:  0     Biog:           MRec:          Ctry:  xx
                     Cont:  b        GPub:         Fict:  0       Indx:  0
  Desc:   a          Ills:           Fest:  0     DtSt:  s        Dates: 1993,      ¶
▶  1   040        NOC ǂc NOC ¶
▶  2   090        Z695.64 ǂb .Y45 1993a ¶
▶  3   090        ǂb ¶
▶  4   049        CLUM ¶
▶  5   100 1      Yee, Martha M. ¶
▶  6   245 10     Moving image works and manifestations / ǂc by Martha Mikkelson
Yee. ¶
▶  7   260        ǂc 1993. ¶
▶  8   300        xii, 230 leaves. ¶
▶  9   502        Thesis (Ph. D.)--University of California, Los Angeles, 1993. ¶
▶ 10   504        Bibliography: leaves 203-230. ¶
▶ 11   533        Photocopy. ǂb Ann Arbor, Mich. : ǂc Universiity Microfilms
International, ǂd 1993. ǂe xii, 230 p. ; 22 cm. ¶
▶ 12   539        s ǂb 1993 ǂd miu ǂe n ǂg r ¶
▶ 13   650 0      Cataloging of motion pictures. ¶
▶ 14   650 0      Descriptive cataloging. ¶
```

Figure 6. Thesis—the photocopy made by UMI

Editions: Brainstorming for AACR2000 51

```
     OCLC:  29424171             Rec stat:     n
     Entered:   19931203         Replaced:     19931203      Used:     19941026
▶   Type:   a     ELvl:   I      Srce:   d     Audn:         Ctrl:          Lang:   eng
     BLvl:   m    Form:   b      Conf:   0     Biog:         MRec:          Ctry:   xx
                  Cont:   b      GPub:         Fict:   0     Indx:   0
     Desc:   a    Ills:          Fest:   0     DtSt:   s     Dates:  1993,         ¶
▶   1   040       INT ǂc INT ¶
▶   2   007       h ǂb e ǂd a ǂe m ǂf b024 ǂg b ǂh a ǂi c ǂj a ¶
▶   3   090       ǂb ¶
▶   4   049       CLUM ¶
▶   5   100 1     Yee, Martha M. ¶
▶   6   245 10    Moving image works and manifestations ǂh [microform] / ǂc by
Martha Mikkelson Yee. ¶
▶   7   260       ǂc 1993. ¶
▶   8   300       xii, 230 leaves. ¶
▶   9   502       Thesis (Ph. D.)--UCLA, 1993. ¶
▶   10  500       Vita. ¶
▶   11  504       Includes bibliographical references (leaves 203-230). ¶
▶   12  500       "93-19938." ¶
▶   13  533       Microfiche. ǂb Ann Arbor, MI : ǂc University Microfilms
International, ǂd 1993. ǂe 3 microfiches. ¶
▶   14  539       s ǂb 1993 ǂd miu ǂe n ǂg b ¶
▶   15  650 0     Cataloging of motion pictures. ¶
```

Figure 7. Thesis—the microfiche copy made by UMI

```
OCLC:    29529046              Rec stat:   n
Entered:       19931220        Replaced:   19931220    Used:       19931220
► Type:    a     ELvl:    I    Srce:    d  Audn:       Ctrl:       Lang:    eng
  BLvl:    m     Form:    a    Conf:    0  Biog:       MRec:       Ctry:    xx
                 Cont:    b    GPub:       Fict:    0  Indx:    0
  Desc:    a     Ills:         Fest:    0  DtSt:    s  Dates:   1993,       ¶
►  1    040      NGU ǂc NGU ¶
►  2    007      h ǂb d ǂd a ǂe f ǂf u--- ǂg b ǂh a ǂi c ǂj a ¶
►  3    090      ǂb ¶
►  4    049      CLUM ¶
►  5    100 1    Yee, Martha M. ¶
►  6    245 10   Moving image works and manifestations ǂh [microform] / ǂc by
Martha Mikkelson Yee. ¶
►  7    260      ǂc 1993. ¶
►  8    300      xii, 230 leaves. ¶
►  9    502      Thesis (Ph. D.)--University of California, Los Angeles, 1993. ¶
► 10    500      Includes vita and abstract. ¶
► 11    504      Includes bibliographical references (leaves 203-230). ¶
► 12    533      Microfilm. ǂb Ann Arbor, Mich. : ǂc University Microfilms
International, ǂd 1993. ǂe 1 microfilm reel ; 35 mm. ¶
► 13    650 0    Cataloging of motion pictures. ¶
```

Figure 8. Thesis—the microfilm copy made by UMI

How Can We Best Link the Editions of a Work?

Now

Currently, for works of personal authorship that are not subject to revision, for translations, for works about which other works have been written, and for anonymous works, we can follow Library of Congress practice and create a uniform title that stands for the work (but many libraries do not, and those that do often have systems that won't display uniform titles).[11] This uniform title can be added to all editions of the work and have the effect of collocating all the editions at one place in the catalog under the name of the principal author of the work or under the uniform title. In effect, the many editions link to the one main entry. A major problem with this approach is that the user, to see all the editions of the work, has to be familiar with this structure. If a search matches on an added entry, rather than on the main entry, the search must be redone on the main entry to be certain all editions, as well as all related works, all works about it, and all works containing the work have been seen. It may be that most users who seek a particular work do happen to search on the main entry (usually the author), but user studies have never been done to examine this question.

Monographic works entered under title or corporate body (other than translations, etc., as above, and other than legal works) and revised editions are linked (if at all) with chained added entries. Each new edition is given an added entry for the main entry of the last edition, if it is different. This is the same approach that is used for serials that change titles. This one-to-one link does not have the effect of gathering all records representing the work together at one point in the catalog. Also, if any particular catalog lacks one link in the chain, the connection is broken.

Because neither of these approaches has been consistently applied, and because they are rather complex techniques, it would be very difficult to program a computer to find all editions of a particular work from the cataloging record for one particular edition.

In order to keep the costs of cataloging down, shared cataloging programs have been developed extensively in this country. However, shared cataloging can have the effect of working against the functions of the catalog. The products of shared cataloging are individual records, an atomized catalog, if you will. These atoms link to each other only when two records contain the same character strings in a normalized heading field.[12] Certainly, we share the creation of authority records as well as bibliographic records. However, the creation of an authority record for a particular author or work does not automatically cause the form of that author's name or the uniform title for that work to be updated in every bibliographic record in which it appears in every catalog in the country. In fact, our national databases and many of our local systems are under very poor authority control. In subscribing to the shared cataloging effort, it could be argued that a cataloging department is taking on the responsibility for maintaining not just its local catalog, but a national utility database and the Library of Congress's catalog as well. Maintaining three catalogs is more work than maintaining one and, even if those three are perfectly maintained, that does not take care of the problem of all the other local catalogs that are not updated when a heading is changed.

The Future

In the following discussion, I would like to make explicit four assumptions:

First, it is still necessary to keep the cultural record (but that record may not include absolutely everything on the Internet). Keeping the cultural record and making it accessible is the professional calling of the librarian. If someone does not take on this responsibility, we are likely to see a new Dark Age beginning in the next century.

Second, artificial intelligence is not the answer.[13] As one computer scientist puts it, "After fifty years of effort . . . it is now clear to all but a few diehards that [the] attempt to produce general intelligence [on the part of a computer] has failed. ... The know-how that made up the background of common sense could not itself be represented by data structures made up of facts and rules."[14] Machines have had a particularly hard time "learning" natural language and "learning" how to do recognition tasks, such as recognizing the nature of the relationship between two entities. Not unexpectedly, efforts in our field to build expert systems have not been very successful. Hjerppe and Olander report on a project that built two expert systems for cataloging; they note that "much of the present cataloging process consists of 'instinctive' interpretation, based essentially on experiential learning from examples in an apprenticeship manner."[15] Among the number of interpretive acts they identify that are difficult for computers to carry out are "the recognition of an item as possibly being related to other item(s) and identifying such item(s)."[16] Humans can perform such recognition tasks nearly effortlessly. For example,

This different name probably represents the same person.
This different title probably represents the same work.
This same name probably represents a different person.
This same title probably represents a different work.

Recognition of the likelihood of a relationship can then trigger research to confirm or deny the existence of one.

What we need is not artificial intelligence but, rather, human intelligence applied toward developing human–machine partnerships that maximize human intellectual input and minimize human drudgery. Just the reduction of the number of catalogs to maintain from three to one ought to increase the "more-better-faster-cheaper" numbers. If catalogers did nothing but identify relationships all day long, they could accomplish much more work in a day than they do now on largely antiquated editing software in many different systems, few of which have been effectively designed to support cataloging work per se.

Third, the term "Information Superhighway" can be translated to mean ubiquitous and cheap telecommunication that could enable us to create a single virtual catalog that would be more like a coral reef built up by catalogers over time, rather than the current catalog model that resembles a cloud of atoms buzzing about, sometimes linking up when they should and sometimes not.[17]

Fourth, eventually we will be able to erase the distinction we make now between system design (indexing and display in OPACs) and record design (MARC and AACR2) and once again take a holistic view of catalog design.[18] Because of this last assumption, this chapter will not suggest specific changes to the rules in AACR2. Instead it will suggest specifications for a holistic cataloging system that encompasses both record and system design. I have attempted to argue here that the problems described are rooted in our cataloging system as a whole, not just in AACR2. To solve them requires systemic change.

With these assumptions in place, I would like to suggest the following specifications for the ideal AACR2000 catalog system that would link editions for users, no matter what the initial search might be. Please remember that the real problem is not the need for mechanical linking devices per se. They are readily available now through hypertext linking. The problem is to devise a method for creating one-to-many links that are sharable, immediately ubiquitous, and permanent.

1. The system would recognize the following six hierarchical levels: superwork, work, version, edition, near-equivalent, and copy. In a sense, this approach is a back-to-the-future approach (see Figure 9).
2. A human operator would be able to point to two records and click on a type of relationship (e.g., same work, same version, different edition; or same work, same version, same edition, different near-equivalent).
   a. This action of recording a relationship need be done only once (i.e., it need not be replicated in multiple databases).
   b. The recording of the relationship will be permanent (but editable).
   c. The recording of the relationship will be immediately ubiquitous (i.e., visible to all users; shared).
   d. At any level with levels below it, a textual label or citation form will be devisable to identify or name the one entity—for example, the superwork, work, version, edition, or near-equivalent—to which subrecords can be linked. This label can be derived from the description of the entity (e.g., main entry [author and title, or title] for the work).
3. As long as local physical collections exist, users should be allowed to limit or prioritize their searches to items that are either locally held or readily available online and that are in particular formats, and they should have ready access to any call number, location, holdings, and circulation information needed to obtain the item or a particular volume or part of it.

   Perhaps in the future we can build systems to maintain electronic documents online as works, with subsequent editions simply appended to the existing record.

SMOLLETT (TOBIAS GEORGE)

—— *See* WRIGHT (Thomas) *M.A., F.S.A.* History of the reigns of George IV. and William IV., being a continuation of Hume, Smollett, and Miller's History of England, *etc.* [ca. 1835].   1500/68.
pp. xi, 627. 8°.

AN ESSAY ON THE EXTERNAL USE OF WATER.

—— An essay on the external use of water. In a letter to Dr. **** with particular remarks upon the present method of using the mineral waters at Bath in Somersetshire, *etc. London: printed for M. Cooper; sold by D. Wilson; Bath: sold by Leake & Frederick,* 1752.   C. 123. k. 3.
pp. 48. 4°.

—— [Another edition.] Edited, with introduction and notes, by Claude E. Jones. Reprinted from Bulletin of the Institute of the History of Medicine, *etc.*   *Baltimore: Johns Hopkins Press,* 1935.   7462. r. 10.
pp. 31–82: plate; port. 27 cm.

THE EXPEDITION OF HUMPHRY CLINKER.

—— The expedition of Humphry Clinker. By the author of Roderick Random. *London: W. Johnston; Salisbury: B. Collins,* 1671 [1771].   C. 95. aa. 8.
3 vol. 12°.
The date is correctly printed in vol. 2, 3.
Anonymous.

—— The expedition of Humphry Clinker. By the author of Roderick Random. The second edition.   *London: W. Johnston; Salisbury: B. Collins,* 1771.
C. 175. m. 15.
3 vol. 12°.   △
Anonymous.

—— [Another edition.] *Dublin: A. Leathley, etc.,* 1771.
1484. bbb. 11.
2 vol. 12°.
Anonymous.

—— [Another edition.] *Dublin: A. Leathley, etc.,* 1771.
1478. e. 41.
2 vol. 12°.
Anonymous. Vol. 2 is a duplicate of the preceding.

Figure 9. An example from the catalog of the British Museum, following rules originally devised by Panizzi. Note that only the differences in each edition are described; portions of the description that are the same as for previously described editions are represented by dashed lines.

—— The second edition. *London: W. Johnston; Salis-*
bury: B. Collins, 1772.　　　　　　　　　12614. eee. 9.
3 vol. 12°.
Anonymous.

—— [Another edition.] *Dublin: A. Leathley, etc.,* 1774.
12612. dd. 13.
2 vol. 12°.
Anonymous.

—— The expedition of Humphry Clinker, *etc.* 1775. *See*
supra: [*Collections.*] The select works of T. Smollet, *etc.*
vol. 7, 8. 1776. 12°.　　　　　　　　　　1578/1925.
△

Anonymous.

—— The expedition of Humphry Clinker. By the author of
Roderick Random.　*London: W. Johnston; Salisbury:*
B. Collins, 1779.　　　　　　　　　　　　1607/4538.
2 vol. 8°.　　　　　　　　　　　　　　　　△

—— The expedition of Humphry Clinker, *etc.*　*London:*
T. Becket; J. Pridden, 1681 [1781].　　　　1607/3762.
2 vol. 12°.　　　　　　　　　　　　　　　△
Anonymous.

—— [Another edition.] *Dublin: J. Exshaw, etc.,* 1781.
012642. pp. 86.
2 vol. 12°.
Anonymous.

—— The third edition.　*London: T. Longman, and G.*
Robinson, 1683 [1783].　　　　　　　　　12650. a. 78.
3 vol. 12°.
Anonymous.

—— [Another edition.] *Dublin: W. Sleater, etc.,* 1784, 85.
1471. de. 44.
2 vol. 12°.
Anonymous.

Figure 9.—continued

SMOLLETT (Tobias George)

—— [Another edition.] *London:* J. *Wenman,* 1685 [1785].
12651. a. 7.
2 vol.: plates. 12°.
Anonymous.

—— [Another edition.] *In:* The Novelist's Magazine.
vol. 19. 1785. P.P. 5262. aa. [vol. 19.]
3 vol.: pp. 197: pl. iv. 8°.
With a separate titlepage, bearing the imprint of Harrison & Co., London.

—— [Another edition.] *Edinburgh:* W. *Coke,* 1788.
12611. cc. 1.
2 vol. 12°.
Anonymous.

—— The expedition of Humphry Clinker. By the author of Roderick Random ... The fourth edition. *London:* T. *Longman;* G. G. J. & J. *Robinson,* 1792. 1607/5216.
3 vol. 12°. △
Anonymous.

—— [Another edition.] *London:* C. *Cooke,* [1794].
12602. a. 5.
2 vol.: plates. 12°. (Cooke's pocket edition of select novels.)
Anonymous.

—— The expedition of Humphry Clinker. By the author of Roderic Random. *London:* J. *Wren, & W. Hodges,* 1795. 1608/5096.
2 vol. 12°. △
Anonymous. The booksellers' names in the imprint are probably fictitious.

—— [Another edition.] *London:* C. *Cooke,* [1799 ?]
12612. de. 23.
2 vol.: plates. 12°. (Cooke's pocket edition of select novels.)

—— [A reissue.] The expedition of Humphry Clinker, *etc.*
[1800?] 1568/1439.
△

58

Some of the plates have been re-engraved.

—— [Another edition.]   *London: J. Walker, etc.*, 1808.
   12613. a. 40.
   pp. xvi, 427 : plate. 12º.
   With an additional titlepage, engraved.

—— [Another edition.]   London: Longman, Hurst, Rees, &
   Orme, 1810.   12651. aa. 28.
   2 vol. 12º.
   Anonymous.

—— [Another edition.]   London: *published for the pro-
   prietors, by* W. Clarke, *etc.*, 1810.   1509/1581. (2.)
   pp. iv, 218 : pl. 5.   8º.   (The British novelists.)
   Published in parts.

—— [Another edition.] (With an essay; and prefaces,
   biographical and critical, by Mrs. Barbauld.)   *London:*
   F. C. & J. Rivington, *etc.*, 1810.   248. a. 28, 29.
   2 vol. 12º. (The British novelists. vol. 30, 31.)

—— The expedition of Humphry Clinker.   *London:*
   J. Walker & Co., *etc.*, 1815.   1568/2308.
   pp. xvi, 427. 12º.   △
   With an additional titlepage, engraved.

—— A new and correct edition.   London: *Dean & Munday*,
   1819.   12651. aa. 41.
   2 vol. : plates.   12º. (Cooke's pocket edition of select
   novels.)
   *Each volume has an additional titlepage, engraved.
   Previous edition in this series,* [1799 ?].

—— [Another edition.]   *London: J. Limbird*, 1827.
   12613. h. 12/12.
   3 pt. :   pp. 159;   illus. 8º. (Limbird's novelists.
   pt. 32–34.)
   Anonymous. Published in parts.

Figure 9.—continued

SMOLLETT (TOBIAS GEORGE)

—— [Another edition.] With a memoir of the author by Thomas Roscoe . . . and illustrations by George Cruikshank. *London: Cochrane & Pickersgill*, 1831.
635. e. 16.
pp. xxxvi, 403: plates; port. 8°. (The novelist's library. vol. 1.)

—— [Another edition.] *Leipzig: Bernhard Tauchnitz*, 1846.
12267. a. 1/302.
pp. 387. 8°. (Collection of British authors. Tauchnitz edition. vol. 92.)

—— [Another edition.] With illustrations by Phiz [i.e. Hablot Knight Browne]. *London: G. Routledge & Co.*, 1857.
12614. e. 17.
pp. 281 : plates. 18 cm.

—— [Another edition.] *London, New York: George Routledge & Sons*, 1882. 12619. i. 31.
pp. iv, 125. 22 cm. (Routledge's sixpenny novels.)

—— [Another edition.] Illustrated by G. Cruikshank, *etc. London: George Bell & Sons*, 1895. 2502. e. 20.
pp. viii, 384: plates. 19 cm. (Bohn's novelist's library.)
"*Bibliography of Humphry Clinker.*" By J. H. Isaacs: *pp. vii, viii.*

—— [Another edition.] With . . . illustrations by George Cruikshank. *London: Hutchinson & Co.*, 1905.
012613. ee. 46/9.
pp. 419: plates; port. 18 cm. (Classic novels.)

—— [Another edition.] With introduction and notes by L. Rice-Oxley. *London, etc.: Oxford University Press*, 1925. 012209. df. 185.
pp. xx, 440. 16 cm. (The world's classics. no. 290.)

—— [Another edition.] With an introduction by L. A. G. Strong. *London, etc.: Thomas Nelson & Sons*, 1936.
12613. b. 27.
pp. xxiii, 453; port. 17 cm. (New Nelson classics.)

—— [Another edition.] Introduction by Arthur Machen. *London: Hamish Hamilton*, [1937]. **012613. ee. 44.**
pp. xvi, 433. 17 cm. (The modern library of the world's best books.)
The titlepage is a cancel.

—— [Another edition.] (Introduction by Howard Mumford Jones. Notes by Charles Lee.) *London: J. M. Dent & Sons; New York: E. P. Dutton & Co.*, 1943.
12206. p. 1/758.
pp. xi, 372. 18 cm. (Everyman's library. no. 975.)

—— [Another edition.] Introduction by Arthur Machen. *New York: Random House*, [1946?]. **W.P. 9139/66.**
pp. xvi, 433. 19 cm. (The modern library of the world's best books. no. 159.)
Earlier publication in this series, [1937].

—— [Another edition.] With an introduction by V. S. Pritchett. *London & Glasgow: Collins*, 1954.
12653. aa. 45.
pp. 352; port. 19 cm. (Collins new classics. no. 632.)

—— [Another edition.] Wood-engravings by Derrick Harris. *Westminster: Folio Society*, 1955. **12651. h. 25.**
pp. x, 371: plates; port. 23 cm.

—— [Another edition.] Edited with an introduction by Lewis M. Knapp. *London: Oxford University Press*, 1966. **X. 0908/46. (8.)**
pp. xxii, 375; map. 21 cm. (Oxford English novels.)

—— [Another edition.] Edited with an introduction by Angus Ross. *Harmondsworth: Penguin Books*, 1967.
X. 0907/15. (21.)
pp. 414. 18 cm. (Penguin English library. no. EL 21.)

—— [Another edition.] Edited with an introduction and notes by André Parreaux. *Boston, etc.: Houghton Mifflin Co.*, [1968]. **X. 909/20503.**
pp. xxxvii, 346: plates; maps. 21 cm. (Riverside. editions. no. B67.)

Figure 9.—continued

SMOLLET (Tobias George)

—— Humphry Clinker ... With an introduction by V. S. Pritchett. *London: Heron Books*, [1969]. X. 909/18350.
pp. 350: plates; port. 21 cm. (The literary heritage collection.)
A republication of the edition of 1954, with the addition of plates.

—— Humphry Klinkers Reisen ... Aus dem Englischen. [Translated by J. J. C. Bode]. Neue Auflage. *Leipzig: Weidmanns Erben & Reich*, 1775. 1607/3175.
3 Bd.: plates. 8°.
Anonymous.

—— Путешествие Хамфри Клинкера. ([By] Т. Смоллет. — Перевод А. В. Кривцовой.) ... Векфильдский священник, *etc.* ([By] О. Голдсмит.) *Москва: Издательство "Художественная литература"*, 1972. X. 989/20191.
pp. 565: plates. 21 cm. (Библиотека всемирной литературы. сер. 1. том 60.) △

Appendix.

—— *See* Brambleton Hall. Brambleton Hall, a novel, being a sequel to the celebrated Expedition of Humphrey Clinker. 1818. 012635. c. 44.
pp. xix, 162: plate. 12°.

—— *See* Dibdin (Thomas J.) Humphrey Clinker: a farce, *etc.* [1831]. 643. a. 2.
pp. 36: plate. 12°. (Cumberland's minor theatre. vol. 4.)
Based on the work by Smollett.

—— *See* Price (John V.) Tobias Smollett: ' The expedition of Humphry Clinker. ' 1973. 011879. de. 2/51.
pp. 63. 20 cm. (Studies in English literature. no. 51.)
☐

Conclusion

These are exciting times. The systems we design now will determine whether twentieth- and twenty-first-century culture will be preserved for the ages. Now more than ever, it is important to go back to first principles and remind ourselves of our goals and objectives. We must remember our responsibility to the many library users, who are mute because they know not how to speak, but who depend on us to make wise decisions so that they can find the works they seek.

Notes

1. Martha M. Yee, "The Concept of *Work* for Moving Image Materials," *Cataloging & Classification Quarterly* 18(2): 33–40; "What Is a Work? Part 1, The User and the Objects of the Catalog," *Cataloging & Classification Quarterly* 19(1): 9–28; "What Is a Work? Part 2, The Anglo-American Cataloging Codes," *Cataloging & Classification Quarterly* 19(2): 5–22; "What Is a Work? Part 3, The Anglo-American Cataloging Codes, Continued," *Cataloging & Classification Quarterly* 20(1): 25–46; "What Is a Work? Part 4, Cataloging Theorists and a Definition," *Cataloging & Classification Quarterly* 20(2): 3–24.
2. Martha M. Yee, "Manifestations and Near-Equivalents: Theory, with Special Attention to Moving-Image Materials," *Library Resources & Technical Services* 38(3): 227–56; and "Manifestations and Near-Equivalents of Moving Image Works: A Research Project," *Library Resources & Technical Services* 38(4): 355–72.
3. My use of the term *version* here is closer to the traditional one than is the current use of the term in the phrase "multiple versions" (for which I prefer the term *near-equivalent*). Examples of traditional definitions of the term *version* follow. The *ALA Glossary of Library and Information Science* defines *version* as follows:
   1. A particular translation of the Bible or any of its parts.
   2. An adaptation, or modification of a work for a purpose, use, or medium other than that for which the original was intended.
   3. One of the variant forms of a legend, fairy tale, or other work of unknown or doubtful authorship.

   Webster's Ninth New Collegiate Dictionary defines *version* as follows:
   1. A translation from another language; esp. a translation of the Bible or a part of it
   2a. an account or description from a particular point of view esp. as contrasted with another account
   2b. an adaptation of a literary work <the movie version of the novel>
   2c. an arrangement of a musical composition . . .
4. The sharp-eyed will have noticed that instead of using the term *manifestation,* which I used in my series of articles, I have used the term *edition.* I do so in the interest of better communication.
5. *Anglo-American Cataloging Rules,* North American Text (Chicago: American Library Association, 1967), 189.

6. International Conference on Cataloguing Principles, *Statement of Principles,* adopted at the International Conference on Cataloguing Principles, Paris, October, 1961. Annotated ed., with commentary and examples by Eva Verona, assisted by Franz Georg Kaltwasser, P. R. Lewis, and Roger Pierrot (London: IFLA Committee on Cataloguing, 1971), xiii.
7. For an extensive discussion of the assumptions about user behavior that underlie these functions (e.g., that users more often seek a particular work than a particular edition of a work, and that users often are unaware of the existence of various editions of a sought work), please see Part 1 of my series of articles entitled "What Is a Work?" It is interesting to note, however, that at the OCLC/NCSA Metadata Workshop, the participants—many of whom were not librarians—when asked to identify 13 key data elements, chose two (relation and source) that indicate relationships between and among documents. (See Discussion Paper 86 in the USMARC Archive, available on LC Marvel (gopher or telnet: //marvel.loc.gov)).
8. Ross Atkinson, "Humanities Scholarship and the Research Library," *Library Resources & Technical Services* 39(1): 79–84.
9. *Guidelines for Bibliographic Description of Reproductions* (Chicago: American Library Association, 1995).
10. John Attig, "Descriptive Cataloging Rules and Machine-Readable Record Structures: Some Directions for Parallel Development," in *The Conceptual Foundations of Descriptive Cataloging,* Elaine Svenonius, ed. (San Diego: Academic Press, 1989), 141.
11. *Library of Congress Rule Interpretations,* 25.5B (rev. Aug. 27, 1990).
12. Character strings that are identical but not normalized can also link. Problems arise, however, when the same character strings represent different entities: for example, two different works that happen to have the same title. Here normalization can have the potential to differentiate two entities with the same character string: for example, using qualifiers such as date of original publication or release, form (textbook vs. play), publisher, and so forth.
13. Hubert L. Dreyfus, *What Computers Still Can't Do: A Critique of Artificial Reason* (Cambridge, Mass.: MIT Press, 1992); James H. Fetzer, *Artificial Intelligence: Its Scope and Limits* (Dordrecht, Netherlands: Kluwer Academic Publishers, 1990); John Kelly, *Artificial Intelligence: A Modern Myth* (New York: Ellis Horwood, 1993); Eric Sven Ristad, *The Language Complexity Game* (Cambridge, Mass.: MIT Press, 1993); and Joseph F. Rychlak, *Artificial Intelligence and Human Reason: A Teleological Critique* (New York: Columbia University Press, 1991).
14. Dreyfus, *What Computers Still Can't Do,* ix, xii.
15. Roland Hjerppe and Birgitta Olander, "Cataloging and Expert Systems: AACR2 as a Knowledge Base," *Journal of the American Society for Information Science* 40(1): 34.
16. Ibid., 35.
17. In March 1995 a discussion of the implications of creating a single virtual catalog took place on the Intercat list maintained by OCLC (intercat@oclc.org); discussants included Hunter Monroe, Charles Floyd Bearden, Cynthia Watters, Charley Pennell, and George M. Sinkankas. Concern has been raised over the potential loss of local practice that can have the effect of customizing a catalog for special local needs. Certainly, it would be desirable for the "single virtual catalog" to allow for different views of the catalog; for example, using different subject thesauri and classifications, even different languages. It has also been pointed out that the idea of a single catalog

is not a new one, that each bibliographic database such as OCLC and RLIN was meant to create a single catalog for many libraries. (For that matter, from the time of Jewett, various attempts have been made to create a single national catalog). It is certainly true that in some sense each national database was meant to form a single national catalog. The problem is that the emphasis was on creating atomized records, not on creating a catalog in which records were bound together by the demonstration of relationships between them. Also, system design assumed as the primary purpose the creation of a warehouse of records from which "stock" could be ordered up using LCCNs, ISBNs, and the like as "stock numbers." The systems were never well designed to support direct user access. On OCLC, for example, it is still difficult to do searches that result in large retrievals; there are no effective displays of multiple headings (e.g., displays that link the editions of a particular work); and displays of multiple bibliographic records are cumbersome, badly arranged (editions don't come together), and difficult to scan through.

18. Although the USMARC format is primarily a communications format, it contains record design rules. Whether or not a particular piece of data is tagged and coded determines whether or not it is readily available for indexing and display in a given system.

What's Wrong with AACR2: A Serials Perspective

Crystal Graham

The shortcomings of AACR2 from a serials perspective can be divided into three major and interrelated categories:

1. The fundamental problems of using book-oriented rules for serials.
2. The difficulty of applying rules designed for use in card catalogs to today's online public access catalogs.
3. The problems posed by new forms of media, such as electronic journals and online databases.

For serials catalogers, the fundamental problems with the second edition of the Anglo-American Cataloguing Rules are structural, philosophical, and practical.[1] Structurally, AACR2 is almost impossible to use, requiring an inordinate amount of page flipping and reliance on ancillary tools. Philosophically, it is grounded in description of the piece in hand, though a serials record must represent issues not held by the cataloger, including those not yet in existence. Practically, title page "sanctity" is a strange concept for materials that rarely have title pages, especially when what substitute for title pages are covers designed to promote newsstand

---

The CONSER Policy Committee invited me to prepare this chapter on what's wrong with AACR2 from a serials perspective. CONSER members and other colleagues were invited to comment on the chapter and I am grateful to the many people who took the trouble to do so. Nonetheless, the opinions expressed here are my own and not necessarily shared by all CONSER participants.—*The Author*

sales. AACR2 emphasizes the appearance of a single issue at the expense of identification of a publication as a whole and its relationships to other publications.

Purpose of the Serials Catalog Record

The fundamental purpose of a serials catalog record is to serve as a gathering device for information about a group of related issues. Kathryn Henderson describes serials as having "personalities of their own." She likens them to humans, who are born, marry (merge), divorce (split), remarry, have offspring, and die. Some are even "resurrected" or "born again."[2]

One might argue that every serial is like a family, composed of individuals. Some are closely related with a common name (and many nicknames), while others change their names and move away. In serials families there are an unusually large number of multiple births, clones, and hermaphrodites that prove troublesome for us catalogers, for we are the serials' genealogists. Relying on the title page of just one issue to describe an entire serial is like using a photograph of just one person to describe an entire family. Often other families have the very same name, so we try to use birth dates and birth places to distinguish them, with varying degrees of success. We need a cataloging code that highlights the relationships and distinctions that exist within and among serial families, instead of focusing on the precise characteristics of any single family member.

Aside from describing the issues themselves, serials records serve as anchors and bridges to related information. In an integrated online system, the catalog record is the anchor for holdings records, location records, circulation records, order records, and check-in records. Perhaps the most popular feature of online public access catalogs is the ability to see holdings information along with bibliographic records.[3] Patrons can find out whether we have a specific issue, where we shelve it, and whether it is currently available. Staff can use the system to keep track of orders, claims, binding, and circulation information. These users rarely examine the entire bibliographic description. They want lots of access points so they can find the correct record and just enough bibliographic data to assure themselves that they have indeed found it.

The bridge function of the serials catalog record is even more compelling. Until recently, patrons underwent a two-step process to find information in journals. First they searched printed indexing and abstracting tools to compile citations, and then they consulted the catalog to find out whether the library owned the journals cited. Now automation enables them to do "one-stop shopping." Indexing and abstracting tools are issued as databases, and software is available to create dynamic links between citation database records and library holdings. Well known among these services are the NOTIS Multiple Database Access Service and the OCLC SiteSearch software.[4] The "hook" most frequently and successfully used to link serial citations and local holdings is the International Standard Serial Number. It is the single element of the bibliographic record underpinning the whole system.[5]

The Cardinal Principle

The intention of AACR2 (and the International Standard Bibliographic Description on which it is based) is to make consistent records for all categories of library materials. The rule makers decided to make serials conform to the monographic mold, rather than basing the serials rules on other standards for serials, such as those of the ISSN System.[6]

The problems for serials begin with Rule 0.24, the cardinal principle, which says, "In sum, the starting point for the description is the physical form of the item in hand." That philosophy is the underlying cause of the AACR2 ineffectiveness in serials cataloging, because of its:

> emphasis on description of a single issue;
> lack of recognition that a serials catalog record must describe items not held by the cataloger;
> failure to place a publication in the context of its bibliographic relationships;
> inability to deal with reproductions;
> inapplicability to electronic media with no perceptible physical form; and
> assumption that original cataloging is always required.

This cardinal principle is difficult to apply to serials because serials catalogers need to describe not just the individual piece in hand but its whole family. Instead of providing information about the whole run of a serial, the AACR2 focus is on a detailed description of the first issue. Any changes reflected in later issues are relegated to the obscurity of the optional notes area.[7]

Bibliographic Description

In AACR2 the bibliographic description for a serial includes much of what John Duke calls "bibliographic minutia."[8] Other title information, statements of responsibility, place, publisher, and physical description are all notoriously volatile. The rules simply gloss over the likelihood of change in these areas. Serials catalogers perform bibliographic gymnastics to accommodate these changes, constantly flipping to the Library of Congress Rule Interpretations, the *CONSER Cataloging Manual*, the *USMARC Format for Bibliographic Data*, or the *CONSER Editing Guide* for amplifications, interpretations, and even reversals of the rules.[9] We need to identify which elements of the bibliographic description are critical and give them a prominent place in the record. As for the rest of the data, we should question the need to transcribe it at all.

The folly of the AACR2 obsession with literal transcription of data from the first piece is particularly apparent in the "numeric, alphabetic, chronological, and/or other designation" area (popularly known by its MARC tag, 362). AACR2 requires that the designation be given exactly as it appears on the piece, in both wording and punctuation. This leads to such unintelligible designations as "1990-1991-1992-1993" when the first and last issues span more than one calendar year. Usually AACR2 uses ISBD punctuation, but in the data contained in field 362, it favors the literal transcription over the far more sensible "1990/91-1992/93" prescribed by ISBD(S).[10] No provision exists at all for recording the designation when the piece is not in hand. The cataloger must refer to a rule interpretation or infer its inclusion from the unformatted designation note included in the *USMARC Format for Bibliographic Data* (field 362 1).

A more serious example of the AACR2 neglect of serials is its failure to provide catalogers with guidance apropos of serial issuing bodies. Instruction is found only in the vague directive to "make notes on statements of responsibility that do not appear in the title and statement of responsibility area."[11] Changes in the issuing body are not mentioned in the rules; the cataloger can only deduce that these changes should be recorded—and added entries provided—from the existence of the 550 Issuing Body note and accompanying examples in the *CONSER Editing Guide*.

Another problematic area is the imprint. The cataloging rules tell us to record in the body of the description only the publisher that appears on the first issue. Subsequent changes may be recorded in the notes area, although the only example given in AACR2 is the exceedingly unhelpful note "Imprint varies."[12] In real life, current publisher information is helpful for identification; it is crucial for acquisitions functions. This information is recorded in myriad local acquisitions subsystems but not in the bibliographic record displayed to the public and contributed to the bibliographic utilities. Alison Beatty and Betsy Humphreys of the National Library of Medicine sensibly suggest using multiple publisher statements to reflect changes in imprint over the course of the publication.[13] This technique is already used, to great benefit, in the *USMARC Format for Authority Data,* where changes in the publisher of a series are recorded in multiple iterations of field 643.[14] In this age of labeled online catalog displays, a list of significant imprint changes, recorded in multiple fields 260, would facilitate identification, ordering, and check-in activities.

Multiple Versions

The preceding examples illustrate but a few of the problems with the AACR2 focus on the single piece in hand. Such problems are even more acute when one has to describe related publications, such as microform reproductions, reprints, cumulations, databases, and imaged materials—what I earlier referred to as "multiple births and clones."

The AACR2 requirement to create independent records for these so-called multiple versions (publications with identical content issued in different physical formats) has generated much debate since its initial publication.[15] As Charles Willard so aptly remarked, the emphasis on the physical format of each version instead of its content is "an obsession with principle to the exclusion of common sense."[16] Although the Library of Congress eventually came to the rescue with a rule interpretation that emphasizes description of the original instead of the reproduction, the requirement to make separate records persists.

This requirement is particularly problematic for serials, because it is common practice for libraries to own at least two versions of a serial. Current issues are received in paper, while the backfile is preserved on microform. Creating "duplicate" records for these publications is extra work for catalogers. Patrons can easily overlook multiple records.

When a large number of these records are included in a single database, such as a serial union list or a bibliographic utility, the separate record approach requires the user, in the words of Todd Butler, "to wade through a sea of similar-looking bibliographic records to get to the holdings."[17] As a result, most serial union lists, including the United States Newspaper Program, use a master bibliographic record with holdings information appended for each version.

Recently, the ALA Committee on Cataloging: Description and Access issued *Guidelines for Bibliographic Description of Reproductions,* which suggests a format displaying all the versions at a glance.[18] The *Guidelines* recommends creation of separate records with coding to facilitate a user-friendly display in the online catalog. In their final report, the CC:DA task force observed that several aspects of AACR2 do not work very well, particularly the cardinal principle in 0.24, emphasizing the physical form of the piece in hand.[19]

Nonprint Serials

Nonprint serials constitute another category where AACR2 fails serials catalogers. Rule 0.24 instructs the serials cataloger to "consult Chapter 12 in conjunction with the chapter dealing with the physical form in which the serial is published." The idea behind the rule is that seriality is a *publication pattern* that can apply to any type of material. Yet, AACR2 does not follow through on that noble premise. The cataloger flips back and forth from chapter 1 to chapter 12, to the format-specific chapter when cataloging a serial map, serial sound recording, serial computer file, serial score, or serial manuscript, but repeatedly comes up empty-handed.[20] The only special provisions, or even examples, for nonprint serials are for the physical description area in chapter 12.

The nonprint chapters never mention seriality at all, resulting in some major gaps in the rules. For example, Rule 12.0B2 says to follow the instructions in each relevant nonprint chapter for prescribed sources of information. Yet not one of those chapters includes a prescribed source for the all-important numeric/chronological designation area.

Computer Files

Of the many nonprint serials, the remote-access electronic journal is one of the most challenging to catalog. Cataloging these serials is rather like describing an apparition with no fixed appearance or permanent address.

Many electronic serials can be accessed over the Internet through electronic mail, telnetting, or file transfer protocol. The cataloger often ferrets for a title in headers, file names, and accompanying documentation. Some electronic serials have no apparent place of publication or issuing body and the Internet address may change without warning. Tracing the bibliographic history of an electronic serial is nearly impossible when its earlier issues have not been archived or when they are stored offline.

While CC:DA was busy developing recommendations for cataloging familiar types of reproductions, a whole new set of multiple versions problems was spawned in the form of electronic journals, the so-called zines. At the ALCTS Serials Cataloging Institute held in April 1995, Regina Reynolds described them as follows:

> They look different, with their hot buttons and home pages and electronic graphics; some of them sound different with their sound files; and some of them, like *Post-Modern Culture,* even sport full-motion video excerpts . . .
>
> Electronic serials are now available as downloadable files, in your choice of Postscript, Acrobat, RichText, Tex, and various other page description or other kinds of file formats. Some of these files, when printed, look exactly like their print counterpart. Now what? Is this a new serial? Does each format need a separate record?
>
> As if that wasn't enough of a challenge, along came the World Wide Web and hypertext files in all of their multimedia glory. Depending on your browser and other hardware and software, *you* may or may not be able to see and hear what I see and hear. Or, you may only be able to deal with the plain text version. How many serials do we have? How can we deal with them?[21]

Other types of electronic journals posing particularly vexing problems are those included *within* abstracting and indexing databases. Nowadays some services include not only citations and abstracts but also the full text of the journal articles themselves. We must provide catalog records for these electronic versions for users, letting them know that the article they want is available online, often through the very workstation they are using.

AACR2 offers no guidance for describing these publications. Not only is there no piece in hand, there is no source of information for the serial as a whole. Who is the publisher? The original publisher of the equivalent print journal? The abstracting and indexing service? The firm leasing the database? The online service providing the search engine?

The only mention in AACR2 of computer file serials is a suggested note to be included in the record for the print version: "Issued also as a computer file."[22]

Bibliographic Hermaphrodites

Neal Edgar, a member of the Catalog Code Revision Committee, declared that the universe is divided into monographs and serials.[23] The structure of AACR2, with print serials off in their own chapter, reinforces this notion. In reality, there are many bibliographic hermaphrodites in the serials family, with some characteristics of serials and other characteristics of monographs. Best known among these is the looseleaf publication, a ubiquitous publication type totally ignored by the cataloging rules. This omission prompted the Library of Congress to issue an independent set of guidelines, *Cataloging Rules for the Description of Looseleaf Publications*, by Adele Hallam. In the introduction to that publication, Hallam explains that the "Library of Congress concluded that by the strict definitions of a monograph and a serial, looseleaf publications constitute neither; instead their unique characteristics need to be considered outside established cataloging formulae."[24]

The gist of the problem is that these publications are issued in successive parts but the end product is a single entity. In effect, they are monographs with a publication pattern. If the title changes, making successive catalog entries would be ludicrous. As Hallam observes, "The cataloger's task is to create a single bibliographic record, not an endless succession of records for nonexistent 'related editions.'"[25]

Online databases also defy the serial/monograph formula. They have serial-like designations and some sort of frequency, ranging from revision at regular intervals to the more transparent "continually updated." Yet, if one day *Medline*, for example, changed its name, it would make no sense to make successive records for each iteration. And what about the databases on compact discs like *The Cataloger's Desktop*, for which each new disc completely replaces the data on the old one?

For years we fretted over whether to use the serials format or the computer file format as we were compelled to jury-rig our online catalog records to circumvent antiquated MARC validation tables.[26] Now format integration will enable us to create MARC records for computer file serials containing all applicable data elements. However, format integration does not provide a conceptual framework for dealing with cumulative databases. The cataloging rules should help us with such critical decisions, but AACR2 is silent. Its failure to provide instructions for such common publication types as looseleaf publications, databases, and other cumulations is one of the major flaws of AACR2.

Unique Identifiers

Another group of rules with serious repercussions for serials cataloging is that concerning choice of entry. Rule 21.1B2 limits entry under corporate body to a few specific cases. For serials, those are primarily works about the issuing body (such as annual reports, catalogs, and membership directories) and proceedings of named conferences. Under the provisions of Rule 21.1C, nearly all serials are entered under title.[27]

The result of this rule is identical entry for unrelated serials with the same title. Some have popular names like *Dialog* or *Vision,* while others have generic titles, such as *News, Bulletin,* and *Report.* Why is it critical to differentiate between serials with identical titles? Lots of books have identical titles and the catalog record serves to distinguish them without resorting to uniform titles. Three important reasons spring to mind:

1. The need to *differentiate* publications in an alphabetical list, such as the review screen of an online catalog
2. The need to *collocate* entries, such as tracings for different series with the same title
3. The need to *cite* serials unambiguously, as in "continuation" notes on successive entry records.

Uniform Title Heading

To stave off the bibliographic chaos resulting from title main entry, the Library of Congress took advantage of the bibliographic contrivance known as the uniform title.[28] A rule interpretation was issued that includes detailed instructions for selecting an appropriate qualifier.[29]

The 1993 amendments to AACR2 belatedly added a provision acknowledging that uniform titles are appropriate "for differentiating between two or more works published under identical titles proper."[30] The rules now include examples of serial uniform titles qualified by place, edition statement, corporate body heading, and date, but they still fail to provide instructions for selecting that qualifier.[31]

The use of uniform title, while solving some major problems, has introduced others.[32] Because the qualified form of title is a uniform title, catalogers are allowed to give only one on a single record. This prohibition means that variant titles, given in the 246 fields, cannot include qualifiers, rendering many into useless, undifferentiated access points.

The Library of Congress determined that a new record should be made when the corporate body used as a qualifier changes name or responsibility. In other words, a new record has to be created even though *the title of the serial has not changed.*

Another problem with serial uniform titles arises when the rules mandate a uniform title for translations. Successive entries are required when the title of the original publication changes even though the translation has not undergone any change at all.

In these cases, the cataloging rules and the concomitant interpretations cause us to "pretend" the titles have changed. Once again our obsession with principle has triumphed over common sense. We would serve our users much better if we allowed qualified forms of title as added entries, representing variant titles, translation headings, and new issuing bodies used as qualifiers. Surely enough confusion is caused by real title changes without us making up even more!

Title Changes

One of the original goals of the Joint Steering Committee for Revision of AACR was to pay particular attention to developments in the machine processing of bibliographic records.[33] That attention should have manifested itself in many positive ways: recognition of cooperative cataloging in automated systems; integration of content designation with cataloging rules; elimination of the redundancy between descriptive elements and access points; acknowledgment of the computer's powerful searching and indexing capabilities; appreciation for the ease of updating a record to show variant forms of title; and provision of mechanisms for linking related records.

Instead, the revision of AACR had the opposite effect. Rather than seeing library automation as liberation from the limitations of the linear card environment, the JSC perceived automation as a constraint on flexibility and judgment. Mike Malinconico articulated this notion in his article "AACR2 and Automation":

> The result seems to be an attempt to reduce cataloging judgment (whenever possible) to precise, mechanical decisions, and whenever possible, prescriptions in AACR2 have attempted to free themselves from dependency on context. When context must be acknowledged, it is done in very precise terms that can be programmed into a mechanical intelligence if necessary.

Whenever possible, prescriptions in AACR1 which required the exercise of qualitative judgment have been made more stringent and mechanical in nature, or eliminated entirely. For example, whereas AACR1 would have permitted one to ignore "slight changes," AACR2 is in general more strict about the treatment of changes. This is very much in keeping with the nature of computer logic.[34]

The number of serials with earlier, later, and other related titles is truly staggering. Barbara Tillett found that more than 47 percent of serials records in the Library of Congress database contained linking entry notes, and that figure does not include absorptions![35]

AACR2 defines a title change as the addition, deletion, change, or reordering of the first five words of the title (other than articles, prepositions, or conjunctions). The 1988 revision relaxed this strict definition a bit, primarily in the area of typographical conventions, but we still require a new record for almost any change in title proper.

Every year, ALCTS distributes awards for the Worst Serial Title Changes, recognizing changes that are silly, unnecessary, and costly. Often these awards are well deserved, but, in other instances, the award should probably go to AACR2 itself for requiring silly, costly, unnecessary, and confusing successive records. Does anyone *really* think we have five different serials when *Atlantic Monthly* changes back and forth between *Atlantic* and *Atlantic Monthly*? In our zeal to achieve consistency in cataloging, we have again abandoned any semblance of common sense. Why not treat minor title variations as added access points to the existing record rather than create a whole new record? Why not regard such variations much as we do variant names of corporate bodies, which are given as references unless there is clear evidence of a true name change? Returning to my earlier analogy, the cataloger should first determine whether what is being dealt with is a member of the immediate family, or whether the new title indicates an extended family relationship. Catalogers should consider such factors as: Is the variation an intentional title change? Are key concepts added or deleted from the title? Has the scope of the publication changed? Did the publication change its numbering when the title changed? Have the typography, layout, and size also changed? Was the serial record created to serve as a gathering device for frequently revised editions of monographs (a purpose defeated by a succession of serial records)?

Not all title changes are silly and unnecessary. Successive entry cataloging should be reserved for intentional title changes that reflect political or social realities, a new focus, or updated terminology. In those cases, successive entries serve us well.

At the very least, we should recognize several categories of changes that can be treated as variant titles. Successive records serve no useful purpose when words denoting frequency change (other than when the word denoting frequency is the only word in the title—for example, Anuario). Likewise, successive records are not useful when a corporate body name is added or dropped from the beginning of a title, when the order of the words changes, or when a word like Series or Collection is added or dropped from a serial title.

A new definition of title changes will succeed only if it is coordinated with the ISSN System. The ISSN is essential for unique identification of titles and exchange of information among publishers, vendors, and libraries throughout the world. It is the crucial link between indexing databases and serials holdings. We must strive for exact correspondence between the bibliographic record and the ISSN, which can be accomplished only by having AACR and the ISSN Program use the same criteria for "major" and "minor" title changes. Compatibility among serials standards will far better serve our users than reliance upon principles formulated for a monographic piece in hand.

Another aspect of the AACR2 fixation with the piece in hand is its limiting the provision of title added entries to those titles physically present on the piece, with a corresponding explanatory note. In real life, users often have inaccurate or abbreviated citations, and provisions should be made for added entries for those variants as well. For example, a serial with an awkward title like *Papers of the . . . Annual Meeting of the Seminar on the Acquisition of Latin American Library Materials* is cited as the more euphonious *SALALM Papers*.[36] Why not make an added entry for that form? The National Library of Medicine reports routinely including entries in their records for serial titles as most frequently cited in document requests.[37]

Surely our priority should be to provide relevant access points, rather than to restrict ourselves to what's printed on the piece. Why is it that catalogers can be trusted to provide appropriate classification numbers and subject headings, but they must include explanations for every name, title, and series access point? Surely patron access is a sufficient justification for any added entry the cataloger wants to assign.

Structure of AACR2

AACR2 is divided into two parts, Description and Access, in that order. The philosophy behind this arrangement is the notion that the starting point for a catalog record is the description. Once the description is complete, access points are selected and formulated.

Isn't it ironic that the rules were changed to mandate description before access at the same moment in history when cooperative cataloging became the norm? AACR2 is written as if every publication were going to receive original cataloging, never acknowledging the all-important step of first searching for existing copy. Obviously we can't look for serials copy without first thinking about access points.

As Fran Miksa points out, "There is really no good reason for distinguishing between 'description' and 'access point' data in a machine system. All data are potentially indexable ... thus making all data potential access point data."[38] The segregation of description and access has outlived its usefulness, especially for variant titles.

As Gregory Wool observes, AACR2 directs us to create records "designed for unlabeled, proselike, description-here-and-tracings-over-there-display—in other words, for catalog cards."[39] The cataloger has to formulate the description according to this obsolete format and then mentally translate the data into a MARC record in an entirely different arrangement. The MARC record integrates description and access, with several fields, like the 246 (variant title) fields, doing double-duty to generate both descriptive notes and added entries. The MARC record is then translated again by machine into an OPAC display with its own limitations.[40]

Practicing catalogers regard content designation as an integral part of the cataloging record. We refer to the areas of the description by their tags, such as field 362, not by the formal AACR2 name of "alphabetic, numeric, chronological and/or other designation area." The current efforts of the cataloging community to define "core records" are couched in terms of the MARC format, rather than areas of the cataloging record. The *CONSER Cataloging Manual* is widely praised for including tagging in its examples. It illustrates how the final product should appear in the MARC database, rather than requiring a second look-up to translate the instructions into the proper format.

A number of data elements carried in MARC fields are not even mentioned in the rules. Many useful fixed-length fields, numeric fields, and even variable-length descriptive fields originate with the MARC format. For instance, services indexing a serial, helpful information for a user with an incomplete or erroneous article citation, are given in MARC field 510. Astonishingly, chapter 12 does not include any mention of this type of bibliographic relationship in the list of notes to be made for related publications.

Catalogers encode bibliographic information redundantly with both MARC tags and ISBD punctuation. If we need ISBD punctuation at all—a questionable premise in an online environment—surely machine-generation from the MARC tags would be a far more efficient and accurate technique than manual input. In 1979, in reference to ISBD punctuation in conference headings, Mike Malinconico remarked:

> One is left wondering whether this was not a solution in search of a problem.... Punctuation, no matter how standardized, is hardly as effective for machine manipulation as explicit content designation.
> ... The net effect is that we now have redundant identification of the various qualifying elements when represented in machine-readable form.[41]

The library community spends countless hours looking for ways to simplify the cataloging rules to speed up production and lower the cost of cataloging. Rather than tweaking the requirements to omit a field here and save a keystroke there, we would realize greater savings with more radical changes: organizing the rules in a logical order, integrating MARC tagging instructions with the cataloging rules, omitting notes that merely justify added entries, and eliminating cataloger-supplied ISBD punctuation.

The Future

So what does the future hold? Numerous authors have suggested that the weaknesses of today's alphabet-dependent linear catalog could be overcome through effective use of automated systems. For example, we could illustrate our cataloging records with scanned images of the covers or title pages of serials to provide for quick identification.

The greatest shortcoming in AACR2 is widely recognized as the "lack of an effective means to convey hierarchical structure and interrecord relationships."[42] Online technology offers new ways to express bibliographic relationships. Members of the LC Serial Record Division have suggested a modular database, called LiOnCat, wherein bibliographic records are connected to related bibliographic records as well as to authority records, holdings records, acquisitions records, location information, circulation records, abstracting and indexing services, and full-text databases.[43]

The Innopac system used in the library at the University of California, San Diego, allows the item record for one physical copy to be linked to multiple bibliographic records, solving the problems posed by binding two or more bibliographic items in one physical volume. This relatively simple capability opened my eyes to the magic of nonlinear relationships. We need to envision information packets with links among them, enabling users to access whatever packet they need at the moment.

Perhaps most exciting to serials catalogers is Melissa Beck's model, which clusters all related serial titles by using unique identifying numbers for each title.[44] An appealing characteristic of her technique is that it results in a schematic that shows *all* related titles, rather than linking only the immediately preceding and succeeding titles as the rules currently prescribe. Catalogers often draw flowcharts of a serial's history for themselves, and I've always thought it was a shame we do not include that chart in the catalog record. Machine-generated diagrams similar to those used in genealogy software would be a great service to those tracking relationships among serials.

Beck's model calls for the use of local system numbers to forge the links. Bob Alan suggests that we take advantage of existing control numbers.[45] All the records in the CONSER database include a Library of Congress control number and an OCLC record number. All records authenticated by an ISSN Center include an ISSN, and many unauthenticated records contain an ISSN transcribed from the piece. The linking fields 76X–78X contain a control subfield ǂw that includes the identification number of the linking title.

Alan's research found that no single number is sufficient to link all serials records. Because not all serials have ISSNs, LCCNs, or OCLC numbers, he proposes a range of choices so the computer can match on any of these three linking numbers. I would add Beck's alternative, a local system number, to be used in the absence of a standard number or to override an incorrect number. An online system could be programmed so that these linkages could be brought together and displayed whenever any title in the group was retrieved—a sort of online family tree.

Martha Yee posits that "the job of the cataloger of the future will be to maintain such links in a local online public access catalog, rather than [to] create the individual records in such a way that they will come together alphabetically."[46] Serials catalogers who supply ISSNs and linking entry fields would argue that we already do that and we anxiously await systems that will take advantage of our work.

Michael Gorman has suggested that in a developed machine system the exhaustive analysis of the relationships between serials that has characterized serials cataloging for many years will, at last, be put to productive use. The complexities that the cataloger unravels will no longer be obscured by the limitations of the card catalog or its derivative, the MARC system. Serials cataloging, always an exact and a demanding art, will become an effective process.[47]

Gorman suggests that the cataloging rules needed to provide bibliographic control in an online environment are much more than revised versions of AACR. He christened his futuristic tool, "The HYPERMARC Record Preparation Manual—Bibliographic."[48] Serials catalogers would welcome such a manual, provided it focuses on identification, coding, and linking of related records.

Earlier I spoke of the serials record as an anchor for dependent records and a bridge to related records. In an online environment we are not bound by such mundane structures but can offer instead magic carpets, in the form of hypertext links, transporting users in the blink of an eye (or at least the click of a button) to related records in the catalog and beyond.

To return to my original analogy, a serial is like a family and catalogers are the genealogists. Our goal is to identify each member and describe its relationships to others. In serials cataloging, as in life, relationships, not appearances, are the essence of family. We're not happy with cataloging rules that tell us how to paste up a photo album; we want instructions for conveying the essence of our serials and building a database of their relationships.

Notes

1. *Anglo-American Cataloguing Rules,* 2d ed., 1988 Revision (Chicago: American Library Association, 1988, with Amendments 1993) (hereafter cited as *AACR2R* when giving specific rule numbers, but cited as AACR2 in the text proper since the defects of AACR2 predate the 1988 revision).
2. Kathryn Luther Henderson, "Personalities of Their Own: Some Informal Thoughts on Serials and Teaching about How to Catalog Them," in *Serials Cataloging: Modern Perspectives and International Developments,* Jim E. Cole and James W. Williams, eds. (Binghamton, N.Y.: Haworth Press, 1992), 10.
3. Frieda B. Rosenberg, "Cataloging Serials," in *Serials Management,* Marcia Tuttle, ed. (Greenwich, Conn.: JAI Press, 1996), 196.
4. Susan Barnes and Janet McCue, "Linking Library Records to Bibliographic Databases: An Analysis of Common Data Elements in BIOSIS, Agricola, and the OPAC," *Cataloging & Classification Quarterly* 13(3/4): 167–69; "New Release of SiteSearch Provides Links from Article to Library Holdings," press release from OCLC, issued on oclc-news listserv, September 7, 1994.
5. In addition to the NOTIS and OCLC systems, Innovative Interfaces, BRS, Rensselaer Polytechnic's Info Trax, and the University of California's MELVYL systems also link databases and local holdings using the ISSN.

6. This system recently underwent a name change from the International Serials Data System to the ISSN System.
7. Alison Beatty and Betsy L. Humphreys, "Serial Cataloging Under AACR2: Differences and Difficulties at the National Library of Medicine," *Cataloging & Classification Quarterly* 3(2): 81.
8. John K. Duke, "AACR2 Serial Records and the User," *Cataloging & Classification Quarterly* 3(2/3): 111.
9. Library of Congress, *Library of Congress Rule Interpretations*, 2d ed. (Washington, D.C.: Library of Congress, Cataloging Distribution Service, Library of Congress, 1990); Cooperative Online Serials Program, *CONSER Cataloging Manual*, Jean Hirons, ed. (Washington, D.C.: Library of Congress, Cataloging Distribution Service, 1993); Library of Congress, *USMARC Format for Bibliographic Data* (Washington, D.C.: Library of Congress, Cataloging Distribution Service, 1990); and Cooperative Online Serials Program, *CONSER Editing Guide*, 1994 ed. (Washington, D.C.: Library of Congress, Cataloging Distribution Service, 1994).
10. Patrick F. Callahan, "ISBD(S) Revised Edition and AACR2 1988 Revision: A Comparison," in *Serials Cataloging*, 257.
11. *AACR2R*, Rule 12.7B6.
12. *AACR2R*, Rule 12.7B9. And you thought the word *imprint* had been eradicated from the rules!
13. Beatty and Humphreys, "Serials Cataloging Under AACR2," 82.
14. Library of Congress, *USMARC Format for Authority Data* (Washington, D.C.: Library of Congress, Cataloging Distribution Service, 1993–), field 643.
15. For a detailed history of the multiple versions controversy, see Crystal Graham, "Microform Reproductions and Multiple Versions," in *Serials Cataloging*, 213–34.
16. Louis Charles Willard, "Microforms and AACR2, Chapter 11: Is the Cardinal Principle a Peter Principle?" *Microform Review* 10(2): 76.
17. Todd Butler, "Sex, Lies, and Newspapers: The Newspaper Cataloging and Union Listing Manual," in *Serials Cataloging*, 177.
18. *Guidelines for Bibliographic Description of Reproductions* (Chicago: American Library Association, 1995).
19. American Library Association, Association for Library Collections and Technical Services, Cataloging and Classification Section, Committee on Cataloging: Description and Access, Task Force to Review Reproduction Cataloging Guidelines, "Final Report," 1993, 1.
20. I thought a serial manuscript was an oxymoron until I was faced with cataloging the captain's log of a ship's voyages.
21. Regina Reynolds, "Paper and Beyond: Cataloging the Evolving Serial." Paper presented at the Association of Library Collections and Technical Services Serials Cataloging in the Age of Format Integration Institute, April 7, 1995, Atlanta.
22. *AACR2R*, Rule 12.7B16.
23. Neal L. Edgar, "Impact of AACR2 on Serials and Analysis," in *The Making of a Code: The Issues Underlying AACR2*, Doris Hargrett Clack, ed. (Chicago: American Library Association, 1980), 88.
24. Adele Hallam, *Cataloging Rules for the Description of Looseleaf Publications*, 2d ed. (Washington, D.C.: Cataloging Distribution Service, Library of Congress, 1992), 2.
25. Ibid.

26. Cecilia A. Leathem, "An Examination of Choice of Formats for Cataloging Nontextual Serials," *Serials Review* 20(5): 59–67.
27. Rule 21.1A permits entry of serials under personal author, but this is rarely appropriate.
28. See Rex Bross, "Saved by the Uniform Title: Would AACR2 Have Worked for Serials Without It?" in *Serials Cataloging,* 123–26.
29. Library of Congress, *Library of Congress Rule Interpretations,* 25.5B, 1–6.
30. *AACR2R,* Amendments 1993, Rule 25.1A.
31. *AACR2R,* Amendments 1993, Rule 25.5B1.
32. For an excellent discussion of serial uniform titles, see Rosenberg, "Cataloging Serials."
33. *AACR2R,* xxi.
34. S. Michael Malinconico, "AACR and Automation," in *The Making of a Code,* 35.
35. Barbara Tillett, "Bibliographic Relationships: An Empirical Study of the LC Machine-Readable Records," *Library Resources & Technical Services* 36(2): 171.
36. Citation from *Hispanic American Periodicals Index* (HAPI) database.
37. Beatty and Humphreys, "Serial Cataloging Under AACR2," 80. The NLM practice was actually to use the citation title as the main entry, not just as an added entry.
38. Fran Miksa, AUTOCAT listserv message, April 6, 1994.
39. Gregory J. Wool, et al., "Cataloging Standards and Machine Translation: A Study of Reformatted ISBD Records in an Online Catalog," *Information Technology and Libraries* 12(4): 384.
40. Few, if any, OPACs can utilize all the complex MARC fields for serials, such as the dual 785 07 fields, designed to display as "Merged with: X , to form: Y."
41. Malinconico, "AACR2 and Automation," 34.
42. Stephen Davis, "MARC Record Wrapper," USMARC listserv posting, April 20, 1994.
43. Linda Bartley, Julia Blixrud, and Maureen Landry, "LiOnCat: Musings about the Library Online Catalog (with a Focus on Serials)," May 1990. Unpublished paper.
44. Melissa M. Bernhardt [Beck], "Dealing with Serial Title Changes: Some Theoretical and Practical Considerations," *Cataloging & Classification Quarterly* 9(2): 25–39.
45. Robert Alan, "Linking Successive Entries Based upon the OCLC Control Number, ISSN, or LCCN," *Library Resources & Technical Services* 37(4): 403–13.
46. Martha Yee, "System Design and Cataloging Meet the User: User Interfaces to Online Public Access Catalogs," *Journal of the American Society for Information Science* 42(2): 80.
47. Michael Gorman [and] Robert H. Burger, "Serial Control in a Developed Machine System," *Serials Librarian* 5(1): 25.
48. Michael Gorman, "After AACR2R: The Future of the Anglo-American Cataloguing Rules," in *Origins, Content, and Future of AACR2 Revised,* Richard Smiraglia, ed. (Chicago: American Library Association, 1992), 92.

Archival Description and New Paradigms of Bibliographic Control and Access in the Networked Digital Environment

Steven L. Hensen

For several years now, I have been delivering to the manuscripts and archival community a simple message: namely, that the information contained within the enormous collections of archives, personal papers, and manuscripts that line the shelves of the special collections libraries and archival records repositories of the world is every bit as important to research and scholarship as the information that is more formally published and bound between covers that fill the rest of the shelves. In other words, archival material (broadly defined) is a legitimate and integral part of the larger universe of cultural artifacts. It is thus both appropriate and desirable that our cataloging systems describe these materials along with other cultural artifacts, such as books, films, serial publications, maps, sound recordings, and graphics. Such an approach serves to strengthen and make more explicit the innate relationship between all these materials and creates within our cataloging systems a seamless web of interrelated research information.[1]

This might all seem obvious and self-apparent now, but convincing archivists and manuscript curators (to say nothing of the rest of the library world) was a difficult task at first. Initially most archivists saw no reason to concern themselves with cataloging at all.[2] This, after all, was something that *librarians* did, and if the rules for library cataloging reflected a fundamental misunderstanding of the very nature of manuscripts and other archival material, it was certainly not surprising to archivists. Instead, it was simply one more piece of evidence in the long case history of antipathy and conflict between archivists and librarians.

Archivists and manuscript curators had labored for decades in self-imposed and idiosyncratic isolation in which librarians were often seen as the enemy of all that archival science stood for. Archival lore and legend is replete with horror stories of librarians breaking up manuscript collections and archival record series according to external subject classification schemes or of removing items based on autograph value or some other artifactual characteristic, all the while utterly ignoring the sacred principles of provenance and *respect des fonds*. Archival cataloging, insofar as it was done at all, tended to be done in libraries that had manuscript or archival collections and was based on the library model, usually focusing on physical or artifactual characteristics and ignoring provenance and context altogether. Moreover, there seemed little hope of developing cataloging or description standards that would satisfy archivists because general feeling existed among them that unique holdings called for unique local approaches and that standards thus never could be applied.

However, the general spirit of bibliographic ferment that was abroad in the late 1970s and early 1980s (which in the library community produced, among other things, AACR2) had its analog in the world of archives and manuscripts. A new breed of archivists was beginning to emerge that tended to take a rather more catholic and less provincial view of their position in the world. They also had a better understanding of the proper place and importance of archives in the larger matrix of research information.

National Information Systems Task Force

One of the most significant developments in this respect was the establishment by the Society of American Archivists of its National Information Systems Task Force. One of the goals of this group was to explore the implications of sharing archival descriptive information in an automated environment. The group fairly quickly concluded that the USMARC format could, with appropriate modifications, easily accommodate the needs of archival description. Although there was some initial resistance to this idea (it was, after all, a *library* standard), it was clear that the fundamental processes of bibliographic control exercised in the creation of MARC cataloging records had their rough equivalencies in archival description. Thus, after considerable discussion in the archival community and with the Library of Congress Network Development and MARC Standards Office and MARBI, the USMARC format for archives and manuscripts control (or "MARC AMC") was born.

It is safe to say that few who were involved in that process had any inkling of the enormity of its implications or of the eventual impact this work would have on the archival world. Virtually no one on the task force understood that, having created a data structure standard in MARC AMC, they also were obliged to come up with a collateral data content standard. Fortunately, AACR2 came to the rescue, if in an altogether unintended way.

Although the publication of AACR2 per se cannot be said to have had much impact on the archival world of 1978, the subsequent archival response to it certainly has. When AACR2 was issued, most of the archival world took little note. Such was not the case, however, in the Manuscript Division of the Library of Congress. As LC was one of the principal partners in the development of the rules, there was a strong sense among the division officers that those rules should actually be used for the cataloging of manuscripts. However, after a brief review it quickly became evident that the rules were written with no obvious input from anyone in the manuscripts or (much less!) the archives community. Moreover, they represented such a significant departure from the rules and principles that were then in use in the Manuscript Division, and at the National Union Catalog of Manuscript Collections, that they were essentially unusable for manuscript and archival materials.

The immediate response of the Manuscript Division (having discovered that the draft with which they had been presented represented a *fait accompli*) was to attempt to develop an alternate set of rules—rules consistent with what were then understood to be sound archival principles, while at the same time working as much as possible within the general overall spirit and structure of AACR2. These alternate rules were thoroughly reviewed within LC by an editorial committee drawn from the American archival community and by a number of commentators from around the country. The result was the first edition of *Archives, Personal Papers, and Manuscripts,* which became the data content standard that made the use of MARC AMC possible within systems whose focus had been heretofore strictly bibliographic.[3]

This manual, now in its second and revised edition, has been widely accepted by the American archival community as the standard for the cataloging of archives and manuscripts, especially in an automated environment. The success of the manual and the degree to which archivists have now embraced cataloging as an essential part of the archival descriptive apparatus has been surprising. It was first intended simply as a useful compromise—a bridge, if you will—between AACR2 and traditional manuscript description that would permit archivists and manuscript curators to catalog and describe their materials in a manner consistent with "non-archives" (that is, books and other library materials), and that would permit the integration of the cataloging of these materials into national bibliographic systems. As the introduction to the first edition of APPM states,

> a fundamental and compelling rationale for this attempt to reconcile manuscript and archival cataloging and description with the conventions of AACR2 lies in the burgeoning national systems for automated bibliographic description. If these systems, which are largely based on the descriptive formats for books and other library materials outlined in AACR2, are to ever accommodate manuscripts and archives a compatible format must be established. This manual is based on the assumption that, with appropriate modifications, library-based descriptive techniques can be applied in developing this format.[4]

The Challenges

Over the past few years it has become increasingly clear that the solutions devised for accommodating archival cataloging, while certainly exciting and important in themselves, also contain within them certain more widely applicable elements that have significant implications for the future of *all* library cataloging. In other words, the difficulties faced by the archival community almost 15 years ago in trying to reconcile the requirements of archival description with AACR2 are not unlike the challenges faced today by the larger library cataloging community as it faces the deficiencies of a cataloging code that is increasingly irrelevant and dysfunctional.

A 1993 article in *Wired* magazine, entitled "Libraries Without Walls for Books Without Pages," noted that libraries are changing from being "fortresses of knowledge [to] oceans of information."[5] Although this was hardly an epiphany in 1993, it is an increasingly obvious and perplexing everyday dilemma in the libraries of 1995.

It seems clear that the implicit rationale behind the AACR2000 conference is that current approaches to cataloging are increasingly perceived as inadequate for managing, much less navigating, this ocean. The new network information model will permit us to directly and dynamically link catalog records to digital representations of the items being cataloged. The focus for libraries is shifting from the delivery of specific titles from their shelves to the delivery of more generalized information from wherever it happens to be. It seems clear that, as the Internet has presented us with an entirely new paradigm for the delivery of information, so, too, must the repositories of that information develop new approaches to information control and access.

To understand how an archival approach to cataloging might be more broadly applicable, it is necessary to go back to some of the problems the archival world had with AACR2. The fundamental problem with these rules wasn't that they failed to understand the essential nature of manuscript cataloging or of manuscript materials as part of library research collections (though they certainly did), or that they had no comprehension of modern archival realities (though that was also true). The real problem was that the very principles of modern bibliographic description were radically at odds with the requirements of archival cataloging.

The *Report* of the 1961 International Conference on Cataloguing Principles (the so-called Paris Principles) still forms the superstructure upon which all of AACR is built. These principles establish the library catalog as an instrument of bibliographic description in which the functions of the catalog are defined purely in terms of: (1) "ascertaining whether the library contains a particular book specified by (a) its author and title, *or* (b) if the author is not named in the book, its title alone, *or* (c) if the author and title are inappropriate or insufficient for identification, a suitable substitute for the title; and (2) which works by a particular author, and (3) which editions of a particular work are in the library."[6] Such an approach, of necessity, places more emphasis on physical characteristics and title page information than on intellectual aspects and content. These principles also contain instructions that "the word 'book' should be taken to include other library materials having similar characteristics."[7]

AACR2 fully reflects these principles and, moreover, seems implicitly to embody the following additional assumptions:

Anything contained within a library ought to be cataloged in that library's catalog.

The records within that catalog and the rules for their creation ought to be structurally consistent in their capture and display of bibliographic data.

Such principles are hard to argue with; there is certainly nothing essentially wrong with them. However, to support this approach, AACR2 goes a crucial step beyond the Paris Principles to assume that *all* library materials have "similar characteristics" to books. Although this was initially problematic with respect to manuscripts (for example, manuscripts and archives do not have "title pages" on which to rely as "chief sources of information"), it has been relatively easy to develop solutions simply through the redefinition of terminology. Some of these solutions in their particulars may irritate the cataloging pedants and formalists among us; however, the solutions have permitted the fuller integration of the larger world of cultural resources and have laid important groundwork for the establishment of entirely new models for information systems.

Location of Material

The problem with the Paris Principles is not that they instruct us to treat everything as if it were a book (though applied literally, this would continue to be a serious problem). The real problem is with their emphasis on creating a physical inventory of materials that is tied to a specific location.

One of the principal difficulties archivists have had with a more "bibliographic" approach to cataloging is the overwhelming emphasis this approach places on the physical and artifactual characteristics of that which is being cataloged. With cataloging based on the formulaic transcription of elements appearing in the *physical* item (title, statement of responsibility, imprint, statement of extent, etc.), the entity is reduced to an object that is identifiable only through those elements. This is the entity as little more than medium. Apart from a very limited number of subject headings and the occasional note (made more and more occasional by the exigencies of backlogs), there is very little in most cataloging records that attempts to convey anything about the *message* or *intellectual aspects* of the item being described. However, this is fully consistent with the Paris Principles.

Not surprisingly, the archival approach is quite different. Because most archival materials are the unself-conscious byproducts of human activity and generally were created for reasons other than those for which they are preserved, they lack the consciously and formally presented identifying data that characterize published works. Thus, there is very little possibility of direct transcription for the purposes of cataloging (instructions in chapter 4 to the contrary notwithstanding). Beyond this, however, there are two more important reasons why archivists avoid a focus on the physical in their cataloging. First, the large majority of archival items exist as part of larger entities, such as record series or manuscript collections (known generically through most of the archival world as *fonds*). Because these items derive their importance and, indeed, their very meaning from this context, archives are almost always cataloged at a collection level. Thus, the implications for an archivist following standard library practices of recording information in the "Physical Description Area" would be to compose a detailed physical formulation for entities that may consist of tens of thousands of items, occupying hundreds of linear feet of shelf space, and consisting of smaller or larger subsets of the entire universe of media upon which information can be recorded. Apart from the sheer folly of attempting this, it is information that is virtually of no utility or interest (except at the grossest level). To the extent that more detailed physical control of the individual components of these collections is exercised, it is done so through a finding aid or collection guide that is prepared separately from the cataloging (and upon which the cataloging is usually based). An approach to cataloging that emphasizes the physical will, perforce, focus on items, and, as already noted, most items have virtually no meaning or importance for archivists outside their larger context or provenance.

Intellectual Content

In 1994 the Library of Congress issued a report of their Information Engineering Analysis Pilot Study Project. The focus of this particular study was to "evaluate the potential value of Information Engineering analysis techniques as a management tool for improving bibliographic products and streamlining . . . cataloging operations." Some of the results of this study, while far from actual implementation, are nonetheless pretty startling. The conceptual framework within which the project team operated contained two major elements. The first, that "LC cataloging should be performed primarily for the benefit of the LC community, with needs of outside libraries and the private sector being secondary," is not terribly relevant to this discussion. The second, however, goes to the very heart of this argument: to wit, "the catalog user is primarily interested in the intellectual content of an item, not its physical characteristics."[8] Although such a statement might be startling to the library world, particularly in light of the historical framework outlined earlier, what is more remarkable still is that it needs to be made at all.

This, in fact, is the very approach that archivists have always taken, albeit as much from necessity as from principle. The focus in archival description is on the analysis of the intellectual contents of the complete entity. Intellectual control and access to archival materials have always been preferred to physical control (or, as John Knowlton, former head of the Preparation Section in the Library of Congress Manuscript Division used to say, "Description conquers arrangement any day!"). As noted earlier, archives lack prima facie defining data and are, furthermore, often highly complex aggregations of primary and secondary materials that may span hundreds of years and touch substantively on scores of topics. Users of archives are primarily interested in locating the information that is buried in these materials, for purposes of either historical research or bureaucratic evidence. The finding aid noted earlier is the key to this and is thus the focus of most archival descriptive work.

It is the job of the archival cataloger to summarize this information and to capture the totality and essence of the material through the judicious use of notes and tracings pointing back to those notes. Thus, archival cataloging becomes "one part of a more complex institutional descriptive system.... In such a system, a catalog record created according to... [APPM] is usually a summary or abstract of information contained in other finding aids, which in turn, contain summaries, abstracts or lists based on information found in the archival materials themselves."[9] This creates a hierarchy of metadata (or, as Richard Saunders has put it, a "hierarchy of surrogacy") with the catalog record serving as the summary-level entry point for increasingly detailed layers of information below it. It is absurd to imagine that the conventions of author-title cataloging with two or three subject headings could even begin to capture the complexity of most archival materials (even if they *had* authors and titles).

Although it remains to be seen exactly how the Library of Congress will refocus its cataloging on "intellectual content" (typically, the report is replete with the usual governmental disclaimers, qualifications, etc.), it at least seems clear that this notion is now abroad with respect to the entire range of other library materials. It is an old cliché with more than a kernel of truth to it that cataloging is often perceived as something that is done more for librarians than for the patrons of libraries. The principal interests of those patrons in the catalog record may still include those enunciated by the Paris Principles for items held locally and physically, but they certainly also include a greater demand for a more detailed analysis of content and subject. Moreover, that analysis can no longer be literally tied to the physical description of a supposed item "in hand."

It would be imprudent to deny that libraries need to maintain an accurate physical inventory of their holdings, but they should not deceive themselves into thinking that in doing so they are also automatically fulfilling the access and research needs of their users. Moreover, as the intellectual entities that populate research libraries metastasize into a bewildering array of new and wonderful physical formats (many of them little dreamed of by the Airlie House Multiple Versions Forum conferees a few years ago) and as library "holdings" become more digitally "virtual" and less constrained by specific shelf locations, it becomes more and more difficult to maintain an inventory in the time-honored fashion dictated by the Paris Principles. It is little wonder that the Gordian knot of multiple versions has yet to be unraveled: Libraries are so tied to the concept of the physical that they have become part of the knot themselves. As physical manifestations of intellectual entities continue to evolve and mutate, the knot will grow tighter and tighter.

As has been suggested throughout this chapter, the archival emphasis on the intellectual over the physical presents one of the answers to this dilemma. However, to take this conceit a step farther, it can be argued that an even more frankly "archival" approach to information management may hold the key to many of the other challenges we face. A brief description of a recently completed project at Duke will illustrate this assertion.

Clearing Backlogs

In 1991, before the ALA Annual Conference in Atlanta, Jerry Campbell, then Director of Libraries at Duke University, was giving an address on improving efficiency in research libraries. In that speech he noted that there was such a considerable backlog of uncataloged rare books at Duke that, if standard rare book cataloging procedures were followed, it would take over 24 years to make this material accessible (assuming, of course, that nothing new arrived during that period). He then went on to announce that Duke was undertaking a project whereby the entire backlog would be made accessible, not in 24 years, but in 24 months! This caught the staff of the Special Collections Library somewhat by surprise, and a Backlog Action Team was rapidly convened and options were discussed and weighed.

It is gratifying to report that during that 24-month period the staff were largely successful in meeting Campbell's challenge. Without going into excessive detail about how this was accomplished, it is worth noting two key factors in the considerations. First, access issues were separated from cataloging issues, in the belief that there might indeed be other and perhaps even better ways to provide access to this material that had nothing to do with cataloging. Second, in looking at cataloging issues it was clear that an approach could not be bound by "business-as-usual" dogma (especially the particular dogmas of the rare book community). Ultimately, the staff knew that they would need to be as creative as possible in their approaches to cataloging, if they realistically were to have any hope at all of meeting the goal.

The centerpiece of this backlog reduction effort was devising an innovative approach to processing the Special Collections Library's Guido Mazzoni collection, which, at over 65,000 pieces, represented a significant percentage of the cataloging backlog. The collection consisted principally of eighteenth- and nineteenth-century Italian pamphlets and monographs and had lain in the Duke library essentially untouched since it had been acquired in 1948. Although there had been sporadic attempts to catalog it, the combination of its size, language problems, and the fact that it was mostly pamphlets had defeated all attempts to bring it under control. This was particularly awkward because it was a well-known collection and contained one of the larger extant accumulations of *per nozze* known to exist in the world. The decision was made to treat this collection archivally.

Because Mazzoni had organized the material into large, generally subject-based groupings, a series of collection-level cataloging records would be created (following LC guidelines on collection-level cataloging of printed materials, which contained much of the same language found in APPM). Item-level control would be provided in a separate database that would be linked to the collection-level MARC cataloging records. This approach obviated the need to go through the entire "AACR2-MARC minuet" with each item since all item-level control was to be exercised within the database/finding aid (where the library was able to make up its own rules!). It also took a distinctly archival approach in maintaining that, however bibliographically significant individual items within the collection might be, what is *most* important is the collection itself. Mazzoni assembled this group of material with specific purposes and focuses in mind and the project, insofar as possible, maintained the original structure in the processing and cataloging of the collection (archivists refer to this as *respect des fonds*). In so doing, perfectly adequate access to this collection was provided without preparing a full cataloging record for each piece. Moreover, developments subsequent to the completion of the project (especially the World Wide Web and SGML markup of archival finding aids) now make it clear that better access to the individual components of this collection can be provided than had ever been considered possible.

Although not all library collections are such obvious candidates for archival control, this model is easily applicable on a broader basis. The key to this lies in accepting two essential principles. First, as was argued earlier, make the catalog record a tool of intellectual access rather than physical control. Second, use the metadata of the catalog record as *an* entry point for access, not the *only* point. Cataloging records in general are currently carrying too much baggage. That baggage is expensive and time-consuming to assemble and, in many cases, isn't even the right baggage.

The Archival Model

The archival model, with its hierarchically assembled layers of progressively more detailed metadata, though postulated in electronic prehistory, is very similar to the hypertext architecture of modern information systems. If the catalog record is redefined as a window or gateway to other dynamically linked information resources, then the structure of that record and the access points that lead to it become something entirely different. In such a system, a search on a subject or name could lead one to a catalog record, which in turn would be linked to a finding aid or some other more detailed form of description, all of which could ultimately be linked to digitized images of actual "stuff"—that is, books, manuscripts, photographs, and so forth. Or a search at any level could lead one to any other level, depending on what one wanted to see. This structure is already at work in the Hypertext Markup Language environment of the World Wide Web. As that structure continues to evolve (which it does on a daily basis), it will almost certainly move toward the more sophisticated and flexible encoding of Standard Generalized Markup Language. Because many books published today are, simply by virtue of the modern publishing process, already marked up in SGML, and, further, because standards are currently being developed for the markup of archival finding aids and other access tools, it does not take a great leap of the imagination to see the pieces of this new information system coming neatly together.

Conclusion

One of the stated reasons for convening the AACR2000 conference (to quote from the program brochure) was to "focus on the effectiveness of the Anglo-American Cataloguing Rules in the face of rapidly changing technology." Clearly, new paradigms of information access and delivery have profoundly challenged the very foundations of library business-as-usual. However, that is only part of the agenda. There is another piece of this story, one that was growing long before the Internet appeared and before anyone had even heard of the World Wide Web. This is the overwhelming challenge posed by cataloging backlogs. The publishing explosion of the past few decades has stretched the technical services capacities of most libraries to the breaking point, even with the economies of distributed cataloging. It seems clear that traditional approaches to bibliographic control are ill-suited to handle the quantity and variety of information resources that are available today. On top of this, the Internet revolution seems only to complicate the issue. Paradoxically, though, it also offers the only real hope of deliverance from the dilemma.

When Sir Anthony Panizzi devised his cataloging principles for the library of the British Museum nearly 160 years ago, it seemed certain that not even he imagined they would stand so long. If he were alive today he would be astonished to see that the "modern" card catalog and its electronic equivalent and, indeed, the very cataloging codes that underpin those catalogs are direct and lineal descendants of the principles he devised in 1836. It seems inconceivable, with all that is known today about electronic information retrieval, relational database modeling and structure, hypertext, SGML, and all the other attendant marvels of the information age, that virtually every research library in the world still relies on an access mechanism that is little more than an electronic version of the nineteenth-century card catalog. In 1991, Dorothy Gregor and Carol Mandel wrote in a *Library Journal* article under the exclamatory title "Cataloging Must Change!" that cataloging "is associated with the application of a set of arcane rules rather than with a set of interesting problems in information retrieval, database design/development, or with managing in a dynamic environment."[10] The questions asked in this article are critical and compelling, but seem to have been largely ignored. The Internet now makes these questions all the more compelling and urgent. It is hoped that the chapters developed for this volume will begin the process of addressing the questions Gregor and Mandel posed and that what is offered here may be of some assistance in solving the problems of information access and delivery in the digital networked environment.

The aforementioned Jerry Campbell is a product of the plains of west Texas and, as such, a great believer in the pithy and essential wisdom of country music. He is well known for quoting lyrics and song titles from that idiom by way of making larger points in various speeches and addresses he delivers around the country. In response to a question regarding country music song titles that appropriately describe the cataloging dilemmas libraries currently face, he immediately responded that an old song by John Anderson fit the bill perfectly. It is called "Let Go of the Stone If You Don't Want to Drown." The image this title summons up is stark and frightening while also fitting quite neatly and directly with the "Ocean of Information" metaphor invoked earlier. Unless libraries have the courage to make the necessary changes in controlling and disseminating the information that is in their custody, they will almost certainly either drown or (perhaps even worse) be beached as irrelevant.

Notes

1. Steven L. Hensen, "APPM and American Description Standards in Relation to ISAD(G)." Paper delivered at International Seminar on Standards for Archival Description of European Archives: Experience and Proposals, San Miniato, Italy, August 1994 (forthcoming in *Archivi & Computer*).
2. I have had numerous opportunities over the past 15 years to speak and write on the subject of archival cataloging. Initially, my audiences were composed largely of archivists or allied professionals who, though originally either indifferent or even occasionally hostile to my message, have gradually come to understand and accept it. In all those years, however, I rarely have had the opportunity to address the library world at large on this subject. I, therefore, want to thank ALCTS and particularly Brian Schottlaender and Daniel Pitti for giving me this opportunity. I also owe an enormous debt of gratitude to the Joint Steering Committee for the Revision of AACR and to the various compilers and editors of AACR2. In fact, in a very real sense I owe my career to them. If it had not been for the problematic nature of chapter 4 with respect to the cataloging of modern archives and manuscripts, I might still be an anonymous government servant toiling in the back rooms of the Manuscript Division of the Library of Congress.
3. Steven L. Hensen, *Archives, Personal Papers, and Manuscripts: A Cataloging Manual for Archival Repositories, Historical Societies, and Manuscript Libraries* (Washington, D.C.: Library of Congress, 1983).
4. Ibid., 1.
5. *Wired* 1.1 (1993): 62.
6. International Conference on Cataloguing Principles, *Report: International Conference on Cataloguing Principles, Paris, 9th–18th October, 1961* (London: Organizing Committee of the International Conference on Cataloguing Principles, 1963), 91.
7. Ibid., 91–92.
8. Library of Congress, "Report of the IE Analysis Project Team," 14.
9. Steven L. Hensen, *Archives, Personal Papers, and Manuscripts: A Cataloging Manual for Archival Repositories, Historical Societies, and Manuscript Libraries*, 2d ed. (Chicago: Society of American Archivists, 1990), 3–4.
10. Dorothy Gregor and Carol Mandel, "Cataloging Must Change!" *Library Journal* 116(6): 44.

Cataloging Uncertainty: Documents, Catalogs, and Digital Disorder

David M. Levy

In a recent paper I examined cataloging practice as it has developed in the modern library era and speculated about its future in the light of ongoing developments in digital technologies, documents, and libraries.[1] The paper was presented at Digital Libraries '95 and was directed at an audience largely of computer scientists and librarians—indeed more of the former than of the latter—and it was meant to serve two purposes. The first was to offer computer scientists a clearer sense of catalogs and cataloging and, in the process, to argue that cataloging is more than just a means of providing access to preexisting materials, as many technologists now seem to think. The second was to offer to librarians, and to catalogers in particular, a view from the outside of one aspect of their work, phrased in language that might be useful in talking to outsiders, computer scientists as well as others.

This chapter is a continuation of these earlier reflections. I will begin by summarizing some of my earlier findings, focusing on four views of cataloging I came across as I was trying to make sense of the subject matter for myself. Following this I will take a look at some of the properties of digital materials that are now up for grabs: issues to do with the immateriality (the intangibility) of digital materials; the problem of determining boundaries between one item and another; uncertainties over the variability and

---

I wish to thank Brian Schottlaender and Martha Yee for help with the preparation of this chapter.—*The Author*

permanence of digital stuff; and the nature of digital genres. I then will look specifically at uncertainties concerning digital surrogates, and in the final section I will offer some observations about how these issues are affecting and are likely to affect the future of cataloging.

The (In)visibility of Cataloging

In a recent article entitled "Making Work Visible, Lucy Suchman notes that representations of work are invariably the product of the perspectives and interests of the people who produce them.[2] What you see, in other words, depends on where you stand and what you care about. As I investigated cataloging during the past year and a half—reading textbooks and articles; talking with catalogers, teachers of cataloging, and non-cataloging librarians; reading e-mail on lists such as AUTOCAT and Intercat—I was struck by the range of views held and expressed about the nature and importance of catalogs, cataloging, and catalogers. I found four of these particularly salient: cataloging (1) as invisible; (2) as mindless transcription; (3) as skilled interpretive activity; and (4) as part of a global system of order-making.

(1) *Invisibility.* This first view, which I myself held not so many years ago, is really the absence of any view or perspective on cataloging. Although most library patrons have some knowledge of and facility with catalogs, they are unlikely to have paused to consider where catalogs come from—how they're created and maintained and by whom. For most of us, catalogs are simply part of the natural order and might as well grow on trees. Indeed, this invisibility is a mark of their success; as Suchman notes: "In the case of many forms of service work . . . the better the work is done, the less visible it is to those who benefit from it." [3]

(2) *Mindless transcription.* In talking with non-cataloger librarians (who wondered why in the world I was interested in a subject so inherently uninteresting), I encountered a second perspective. Cataloging, I discovered, is viewed in some quarters as a form of mindless transcription, a rote transfer of bibliographic properties from items to catalog records. I later found this view neatly summarized (albeit somewhat tongue-in-cheek) in a column entitled "Catalogers, We Hardly Know Ye":

> But to many of us in the [library] profession, catalogers remain an unfathomable mystery. Unable to understand the fires of dedication that burn brightly within them, we often poke fun at their internecine controversies. To those of us who are on the firing line of big issues

like intellectual freedom and library funding, the wars waged by catalogers over the future of the main entry or the role of the hyphen often appear to be peevish squabbles fought by socially dysfunctional nitpickers.

Where did catalogers come from we often wonder. Theories, of course, abound. Some speculate that they are aliens from a faraway galaxy who have come to earth to tidy things up a bit. Others believe that catalogers may be the descendants of the lost tribe of Israel. After all, they point out, there is a very close similarity between the book of Deuteronomy and AACR2.[4]

(3) *Skilled interpretive activity.* I came to this third view as I tried to make sense of cataloging from the inside, from the perspective of working catalogers (insofar as I could do this without actually practicing the art). In reading textbook material and journal articles, but most especially in listening in on catalogers' conversations on AUTOCAT and Intercat, I caught a glimpse of cataloging not as a process of mindlessly transcribing bibliographic properties, but one of normalizing or regularizing the target material to conform to standard categories of description, a process of making the properties in the very act of describing them. I saw that in performing the supposedly routine work of cataloging, the cataloger is constantly called upon to make decisions requiring considerable skill and judgment: Is this work a monograph or a serial? Who is the author? Is this work the same as that one? What is the subject of this work?

(4) *Part of a global system of order-making.* Although the fourth view of cataloging is a broadening and an elaboration of the third, it is probably more the perspective of a theoretician than that of a cataloging practitioner. In this view, cataloging is part of the global system of order-making that Roger Chartier has called "the order of books."[5] This is the system of institutions (publishers, libraries, booksellers), genres (novels, pamphlets, newspapers), surrogates (catalog records, bibliographic entries, finding aids), categories of description (author, work, edition), and government regulation (copyright) that has evolved over centuries to stabilize and make accessible the flood of bibliographic materials "that first the manuscript book and then print put into circulation."[6] From this point of view, cataloging is to be understood in relation to, and inseparable from, a range of other activities, including writing, publishing, editing, selling, and reading.

No doubt there is some truth in all four of these views. But if we are to look for help in predicting or assessing cataloging's future, we will probably get more leverage from the third and fourth perspectives than from the first and second. For these latter two perspectives suggest that insofar as cataloging is concerned with affording access to bibliographic materials, it is a much more intellectually challenging activity than generally thought; and beyond this, that cataloging is concerned with more than (just) providing access to bibliographic materials, that it is an integral part of the system by which these materials are constructed and maintained. And this suggests further that discussions of its future will need to be framed in terms broader than access, perhaps in terms of the stability of the entire bibliographic universe.

Dimensions of Digital Uncertainty

Of course, the stability of the bibliographic universe is now very much in question. We are no longer sure whether the "order of books"—an order based on one central artifact, the codex, and its derivatives—will hold up. Indeed, the future of virtually all the elements I mentioned earlier is now unclear: the nature of publishing, of future genres, of surrogates, and so on. As far as cataloging practice is concerned, one of the main uncertainties must be about the nature of digital material. What exactly is it that catalogers will catalog? Although it is too early to answer this question, I think it is still possible to say something concrete by, in effect, factoring the uncertainty and identifying five more specific loci of uncertainty: (1) materiality, (2) boundaries, (3) variability, (4) permanence, and (5) genre.

(1) *Materiality.* One of the terms frequently used to characterize digital materials is *virtual,* which is meant to set them in opposition to the physical, tangible nature of paper-based documents. Whereas books have weight and size and location, digital materials seem somehow to be insubstantial and intangible. The ease and frequency with which the term *virtual* is invoked, however, should not mask the underlying uncertainty about exactly what we mean by it. Part of what is being pointed to is the separation that digital technology has effected between the underlying representation of a document (stored, say, on a file server) and the perceptible forms realized from it on screens and on paper.[7] Increasingly we seem to be taking the former, which is inherently invisible and intangible, to be the "real" document, while the latter, the visible, tangible manifestations, are taken to be transitory and of secondary importance. In this way, digital material seems to have come unmoored from the material foundation of earlier document forms.[8]

(2) *Boundaries.* One consequence of this dematerialization is the loss of boundaries between items, or at least uncertainty about how such boundaries are to be determined. In the domain of print and paper, books acquire their boundaries directly from their materiality; they are relatively discrete, bounded objects. But the current state of the Internet and the Web suggests a future digital universe made up not so much of discrete entities as of highly interlinked fragments with no clear boundaries between one item (should one even say "document"?) and another.[9] As Geoffrey Nunberg comments, "Reading what people have had to say about the future of knowledge in an electronic world, you sometimes have the picture of somebody holding all the books in the library by their spines and shaking them until the sentences fall out loose in space."[10]

(3) *Variability.* Another uncertainty concerns the rate at which digital materials will change. There is a pervasive sense that digital materials will be more variable than their print/paper counterparts. The ease of copying and modifying digital materials, for example, means that documents can be customized to suit individuals or groups. Does this spell the end of one of the mainstays of print culture, the notion of edition? Certain kinds of digital documents—spreadsheets, for example—are becoming more dynamic, more interactive, and even programmable, suggesting that they may need to be treated more like active processes than fixed materials. How such forms of variability will eventually stabilize is far from certain.

(4) *Permanence.* Although we have a pretty clear understanding of the durability and permanence of paper and other tangible media, it is not so clear how to assess the expected lifetime of digital materials. There are multiple issues here. One is simply the survival of the physical media—floppy disks, CDs, tapes, and so on—as well as of the hardware and software needed to access documents stored on these media. To judge from the recent past, documents stored in digital media cannot be expected to be (easily) available for more than a decade. The permanence of documents, however, is as much a social as a technological question. The survival of Greek and Roman classics, for example, has only partly to do with the durability of vellum and paper; it has equally to do with the social practices of copying and critically editing texts. We have to assume that the survival of digital materials will be equally a matter of social and technical design. The bigger question is: How long will we want digital materials to survive?

(5) *Genre.* Questions such as this last one, however, cannot be answered with respect to digital documents as a whole. Instead, the proper level at which to address them is that of genre. Indeed, all four of the preceding

issues are probably best located at this level, because the class or type of a document is the place where form, content, and use are bound together.[11] Right now there is very little clarity about digital genres. Whereas a vast number of genres have developed for paper- and print-based materials over the centuries, there are as yet very few of the digital variety. Until quite recently, most digital materials have aped long-standing paper-based genres; we have created digital memos, journals, calendars, and so on. Even developments such as multimedia and hypertext, which have been taken to be truly novel digital genres, are really new technologies from which new genres (e.g., home pages?) may eventually emerge.

The Uncertainty of Digital Surrogates

Thus far I have focused on the status of what might be called primary materials, and I have commented on some of the uncertainties surrounding these as they increasingly take digital form. But we might also inquire about the status of secondary materials as they too take digital form. In Figure 1 I have depicted two information domains, labeled "primary materials" and "secondary materials." Primary materials are the books and serials, the videotapes and online journals that people search out, browse, and read, and which catalogers (now or in the future) catalog. By secondary materials I mean the range of surrogates—catalog records, URLs, whatever—that refer to and are used to organize and provide access to primary materials.

It is interesting to observe how the material composition of these two domains has been changing in recent decades. Until roughly 1980, the vast majority of materials in both domains was realized in paper form. Beginning in the 1980s with the development and wide-scale adoption of OPACs, a significant proportion of one class of secondary materials, catalog records, began to migrate to digital form. Only in the past few years have we begun to see an important selection, if not a substantial proportion, of primary materials appear in digital form. (It is interesting to note that secondary materials actually made the transition first and that libraries were in the vanguard.)

What can be said about the status of secondary materials in digital form, about the status of digital surrogates? My main observation is that they are subject to the same kinds of uncertainty as are primary digital materials; that is, issues of materiality, boundaries, variability, permanence, and genre arise equally for secondary as for primary materials.

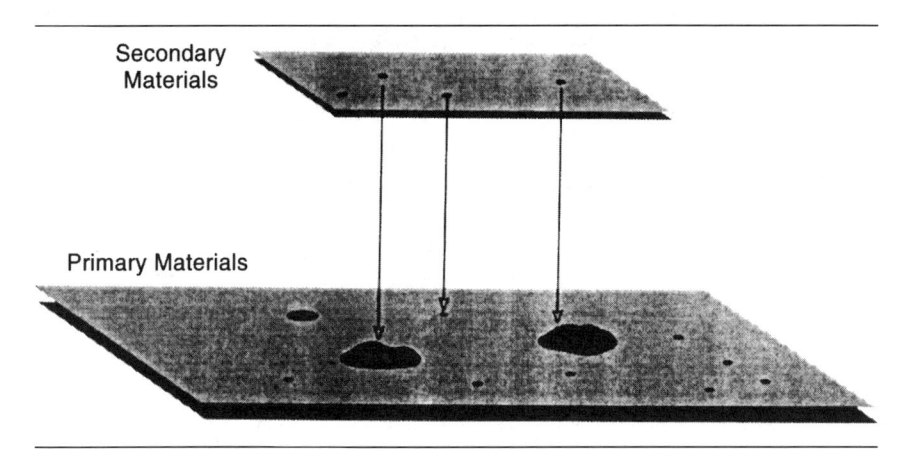

Figure 1. The bibliographic universe consisting of primary and secondary materials. Arrows indicate that a secondary item (e.g., a catalog record) refers to and describes a primary item (e.g., a book or work).

Take the question of materiality and boundaries. In a world of richly interlinked digital materials, it may no longer be so clear where one surrogate begins and another one ends. Equally, the boundary between a surrogate and that for which it stands may be hard to discern: The distance between surrogates and items may be shrinking. Notice how on the Web there has been an explosion of surrogates—currently URLs and shortly URNs—and how these are directly embedded in the primary material. Thus a strong distinction between primary and secondary materials based on physical boundaries may be hard to maintain. Notice too that the Text Encoding Initiative has proposed that an elaborate header, something like a catalog record, be part of the document it describes. (The larger point, of course, is that in a world of digitally linked materials, the notion of "part of" is bound to undergo some revision.)

The variability and permanence of digital surrogates are also uncertain. It is well known that paper- and film-based catalog records have been difficult and expensive to modify, while digital equivalents have the potential, at least, to be more malleable. The hope is that digital surrogates will be responsive to changes in the materials they describe, although what combination of technical and social means this will require is not yet clear. There are also questions about how variable digital surrogates should be that parallel questions about the variability of primary digital materials. If, for example, customized records can be created in response to a user's query, how long, and in what form, should they remain in existence?

Finally, it is not yet clear what new genres of digital surrogates will come into existence or what changes older ones will undergo. The MARC record came about as a fairly straightforward clothing of a paper-based genre in digital form. Does anyone seriously doubt that its days are numbered? URLs, URNs, and URCs are newly emerging forms, but even these are closely wedded to earlier forms.[12] As with digital primary materials, there are as yet no mature genres of digital surrogates.

The Future of Cataloging

However these uncertainties are resolved, it seems clear that surrogates in the digital domain will not only survive but prosper: There will be more surrogates than ever before. But where, you might ask, does all this leave cataloging? Thus far, answers to this question have been framed largely in terms of access. On one extreme is the suggestion that cataloging will be made obsolete by powerful search tools and intelligent agents—we'll be able to find what we're looking for without the intermediation of human-prepared catalogs. The response to this has been an equally extreme conservatism—things work as they are, thank you, and if it ain't broken, don't fix it.

But like it or not, something does seem to be broken. What is happening now is more than just the addition of some (as yet ill-defined) new genres, but a readjustment of some proportion of the entire information order. What is at issue is more than just the means of obtaining access to this information; it is the active construction and maintenance of the information and its attendant institutions and practices. It is my sense that the future of cataloging must be assessed in this broader context.

Earlier in this chapter, I observed that cataloging is a skilled interpretive activity that is part of the system for constructing and stabilizing materials. Framing it this way raises important questions beyond "mere" access: In the future, how—through what institutions, professions, and practices—will digital materials be constructed and maintained? To what extent will this work, or even could this work, be automated, and to what extent will it require the intervention of skilled professionals? To the extent that skilled intervention is required—and it seems virtually certain to me that some amount is inevitable—will this work be thought of as "cataloging" or even viewed as an outgrowth of earlier cataloging practices?

These are major social and political questions and are not simply reducible to technological decisions. It is crucial that catalogers, concerned to protect their profession as well as the values and knowledge that underlie it, participate in the emerging dialogue about the future of libraries and find ways to represent and make visible their skills and knowledge. The task, it seems to me, will be to make clear how current practices are a form of order-making, and to do this in ways that don't appear to equate these practices with structures that are bound to change and possibly disappear, such as MARC records and AACR2.

Notes

1. David M. Levy, "Cataloging in the Digital Order," in *Proceedings of Digital Libraries '95: The Second Annual Conference on the Theory and Practice of Digital Libraries, June 11–13, 1995, Austin, Texas*, Frank M. Shipman, Richard Furuta, and David M. Levy, eds. (College Station, Tex.: Hypermedia Research Laboratory, 1995), 31–37.
2. Lucy Suchman, "Making Work Visible," *Communications of the ACM* 38(9): 56–64.
3. Ibid., 58.
4. Will Manley, "Catalogers, We Hardly Know Ye," *American Libraries* 25(7): 661.
5. Roger Chartier, *The Order of Books: Readers, Authors, and Libraries in Europe between the Fourteenth and Eighteenth Centuries* (Stanford, Calif.: Stanford University Press, 1994).
6. Ibid., vii.
7. David M. Levy, "What Do You See and What Do You Get? Document Identity and Electronic Media," in *Screening Words: User Interfaces for Text. Proceedings of the Eighth Annual Conference of the UW Centre for the New OED and Text Research* (Waterloo, Ont.: UW Centre for the New OED and Text Research, 1992), 109–17.
8. Geoffrey D. Nunberg, "The Places of Books in the Age of Electronic Reproduction," *Representations* 42 (1993): 13–37.
9. Of course, if this comes about, it won't be the first time in our culture that we have encountered—or perhaps one should say constructed—immaterial bibliographic entities with fuzzy boundaries. Works, as opposed to books, are themselves fuzzy, abstract things whose boundaries are culturally determined and maintained on an ongoing basis. Indeed, copyright and the courts are part of the system, as are catalogers, by which the boundaries between works are negotiated.

    Though we may tend to think of the work as a natural and fixed category, recent historical scholarship has begun to trace its evolution. In *Authors and Owners* (Harvard University Press, 1993), for example, Mark Rose shows how, within the legal system, the abstract notion of the work came to take precedence over books and other tangible, physical artifacts as the locus of ownership and other rights.
10. Nunberg, "The Places of Books," 22.
11. Because the term *genre* is used somewhat differently in different disciplines, I will briefly elaborate:

    The central observation is that documents come to us not as isolated artifacts but as instances of recognizable social types or genres—e.g., as novels, packing receipts, shopping lists, journal articles, and so on. These types, typically arising out of a particular constellation of technologies (e.g., the newspaper from press and paper), classify documents primarily according to their purpose. That is, each genre brings together a particular form with a particular set of functions or roles; indeed, it allows us, to a large measure, to recognize the intended purpose and institutional role of a document from the form alone and thereby gives us a context for interpretation. This is a highly efficient way of conveying a great deal of information. Thus, one does not need a user manual to know how to read a newspaper. An understanding of the relationship between size of headline or placement on the page and importance of article, the ability to differentiate the rhetoric of a front-page story from that of an op-ed article, an understanding of the relationship(s) between the stories and the various institutions, such as the news gathering agencies, associated with them—all this is part of the tacit background shared by literate members of the culture. (David M. Levy, "Fixed or Fluid?: Document Stability and New Media," in *European Conference on Hypermedia Technology, 1994: Proceedings* [New York: Association for Computing Machinery, 1994], 25.)

12. David M. Levy, "Naming the Nameable: Names, Versions, and Document Identity in a Networked Environment," in *Scholarly Publishing on the Electronic Networks: Filling the Pipeline and Paying the Piper: Proceedings of the Fourth Symposium: November 5–7, 1994, the Washington Vista Hotel, Washington, D.C.,* Ann Okerson, ed. (Washington, D.C.: Association of Research Libraries, 1995), 153–59.

Bibliographic Description and Digital Objects: Toward a New Discipline of Information Description and Management

Clifford Lynch

Both the context and the nature of cataloging are changing. Until this decade, the vast majority of cataloging has dealt with the control of physical artifacts. Although there have been controversies of a highly specialized nature (such as those leading up to format integration), the basic principles and objectives of cataloging have remained remarkably stable. Similarly, the library community has enjoyed two decades of relatively constant technical context: The primary medium of creation, transport, and use of cataloging data has been the MARC record. MARC records are either created or selected from centralized cataloging databases and imported into local integrated systems where they form the institutional databases that serve patrons as online catalogs. The gradual but massive shift to national-level copy cataloging (and the emergence of such recent developments as the direct supply of catalog records along with books from publishers and vendors) has led to a more uniform base of cataloging across libraries—in effect, mass-production cataloging to match mass-production publishing—and there are fewer individuals today skilled in the practice of original cataloging. The increasingly centralized nature of cataloging means that changes in practice can probably take place more rather than less rapidly in the future.

Currently, the focus on the fundamentally new issues involved in describing, organizing, and managing networked information resources and other digital objects is stimulating a reconsideration of a number of assumptions. These are not mass-produced and mass-replicated (published) objects; they are unique, yet widely used and shared. Their relationship to traditional library collections and to library processes of acquisition, organization, and preservation is still unclear. "Metadata"—data that accompany these digital objects and resources and support their use and management—has become an extremely popular topic of discussion, though one which does not seem to be well understood or well defined. At times, it seems that the term *metadata* is being used simply as a more fashionable and sophisticated-sounding synonym for descriptive cataloging of digital information, perhaps with some hope that tomorrow's metadata specialist will gain greater recognition and reward than today's librarian/cataloger. In my view, this conceptualization of metadata misses the significance of the developments that are taking place. Traditional descriptive cataloging is becoming more clearly placed as just one of a multiplicity of approaches to describing information resources, and this entire range of resource description techniques (including, as well, subject cataloging) forms only a part of the emerging range of metadata that is being recognized as necessary to facilitate the use and management of digital objects and resources.

The systems context, not merely for creation of cataloging data but more importantly for the application of these data in location, selection, and use of networked information—"networked information discovery and retrieval," or NIDR, as it is sometimes termed—is highly unstable, with new technological approaches both emerging and becoming obsolete at a rapid pace. While still unstable, this context is clearly very different from the predictable world of an online catalog that described well-understood physical objects held in a library.

User expectations and requirements are evolving as well, and there is, I believe, a growing recognition that cataloging and related practices will have to evolve in response to these new user needs rather than being limited by abstract ideas about the goals of the cataloger's art. Indeed, the networked environment is a competitive one, with library-based and various forms of commercial services competing on a much more equal footing than in the past to serve those seeking information. In a time of continually diminishing budgets, economic questions—in particular, questions of cost justification and cost–quality trade-offs—are increasingly being raised in relation to continued large-scale investment in traditional cataloging approaches.

This chapter briefly surveys some aspects of this changing context for cataloging practice. It is not intended to be comprehensive or definitive, but only to suggest important trends that need to be considered in thinking about the future of cataloging and the use of cataloging information. While the chapter is loosely based on a paper that I delivered at the AACR2000 Conference in 1995, it is expanded to consider some developments through mid-1996.

Cataloging Becomes Fungible

Historically, cataloging has been driven by three standards. The *Anglo-American Cataloguing Rules,* second edition, establishes how to define various data elements for a work; MARC assigns fields and tagging (detailed structure) to these data elements; and Z39.2 provides the specific interchange format to carry the MARC-tagged fields. The boundaries between these standards—particularly that between AACR2 and MARC—are not as clear and modular as one might like, but, because they were always used together, the definition of the bibliographic records produced by this complex of standards was not jeopardized. Indeed, these standards are a tribute to the effectiveness of a community-wide program of data definition for interchange and stand as an example for other communities (particularly in some of the sciences) that are currently attempting to develop community data interchange standards.

Recently, new interchange formats (SGML Data Type Definitions and ASN.1 structures) have been proposed as alternatives to the Z39.2 encoding that historically has been used to carry MARC records. Although disconcerting to some traditionalists, the impact of these proposals is relatively small because the new encodings can be algorithmically translated to and from Z39.2 encodings. They represent a very real coding problem but not much of a conceptual one. Other developments are taking place that are more problematic, however.

Before about 1993, traditional descriptive and subject cataloging (as defined by AACR2 and MARC) remained within MARC records; the data elements were reformatted only for transient screen display in online catalog systems. (These screen displays themselves became specialized interchange formats between personal-computer–based bibliography managers and online catalog databases in an ad hoc fashion. Work is now underway on a formal standard for the use of tagged displays for downloading into personal bibliography managers under NISO auspices; this should reduce the need for such bibliography managers to provide special import programs for various individual online catalogs.) The mapping of a MARC record to a display format is not invertable; it discards information.

Recently, matters have become much more fluid. A number of structured record formats—for example, various SGML Document Type Definitions, including the markup developed by the Text Encoding Initiative or the Federal Geographic Data Committee metadata format—contain numerous fields that might be algorithmically interchanged with similar fields within MARC records. There is not a one-to-one match: Each of these formats contains data elements that do not appear (at least commonly or explicitly) within the MARC record, and none can accommodate conveniently all the fields that might appear in a MARC record. Data element semantics are similar, but not necessarily identical across the various formats.

We are now in a world where data elements can move freely, dynamically, and computationally from one carrier structure and context to another, and where MARC records themselves can be embedded (in their entirety, as subobjects) in much more complex interchange and storage structures. In most cases, these data elements describe electronic rather than physical objects, and the semantics of the data elements are not always completely clear or consistent from structure to structure. We have not yet begun to consider the maintenance ramifications of this dispersion and computational replication of data elements over long periods of time (for example, how to do authority control maintenance in such an environment). There is now a multiplicity of descriptions, both external to electronic objects and embedded within them. The issue is how to produce and maintain these various descriptions with a minimum of effort.

Recombinant Description and Classification

The basic assumption underlying AACR2 and MARC is that a trained cataloger will invest considerable intellectual effort in describing a work. AACR2/MARC requires a cataloger to make a number of careful distinctions and thoughtful decisions in creating a descriptive record or assigning subject headings. Catalogers in this world are supported by increasingly sophisticated record creation and editing systems (such as the OCLC or RLG online cataloging systems today, and the cataloger's workstations currently under development) that permit them to build and modify the elaborate interchange formats defined by MARC/AACR2. These support systems do not today include features for automatic extraction of algorithmically derivable data elements; they are still designed under the assumption that they are serving a cataloger who has the physical object to be cataloged in his or her hands.

In the networked information environment, which facilitates rapid and highly distributed "publication" of information, there has been a great deal of interest in developing descriptive schemes that permit relatively casual description of objects (for example, by authors, site administrators, or other individuals untrained in cataloging). There are two motivations for this: timeliness (the ability to prepare description concurrent with the act of publication) and management of costs (presumably it will be much less expensive for nonspecialists to do superficial description of materials). A variety of these simple descriptive schemes are in use or under development, including the descriptive format developed as part of the ARPA-funded Computer Science Technical Report project and efforts related to the Dublin Core Metadata set. While establishing some of the data elements in these schemes still requires intellectual effort, many of them can be extracted computationally from structured electronic documents directly, without human intervention.

Most of these approaches do not use classification in the traditional sense. Rather, they rely on uncontrolled keywords for access or computed keywords or phrases derived from author abstracts, or even the full text of the documents in question. Whatever structure may be provided in subject access is obtained through computation and statistical methods rather than intellectual design of a subject terminology.

These new schemes are "simpler" than MARC/AACR2 in two distinct senses. First, they are intended to be used, as indicated, by minimally trained or untrained "catalogers"—the intellectual effort to create records under these schemes is intended to be reduced and, at least in theory, can be minimized by systems that capture many of the data elements directly from the electronic versions of the objects being described. Second, they often employ much more basic record interchange formats. The ARPA Computer Science Technical Report records, for example, were designed so that they could be created using any text editor or e-mail package (though at the expense of not automatically extracting those data elements that can be extracted automatically and of not validity-checking the format of the created records—features that would require that the text editor be supplemented by some custom macros or scripts). Over the past year there has been work on standards to allow authors to include elements from the Dublin Core Metadata set in HTML documents by simply adding some additional HTML META tags.

These lower-quality descriptive schemes are not intended to replace traditional cataloging as defined by AACR2/MARC, though for specific classes of works the simpler descriptions are intended to serve as either temporary or permanent substitutes for more time-consuming and costly traditional cataloging. One question that nobody seems eager to explore is a quantification of the cost-benefit trade-offs between these simpler schemes and traditional "full-quality" cataloging.

An environment that mixes descriptive approaches of varying depth and quality and that is populated by a mix of retrieval and management systems predicated upon different levels of descriptive records raises a host of questions that are just now beginning to be explored. Clearly, high-quality descriptive records can be downgraded algorithmically to the simpler formats. However, simpler records cannot easily be upgraded without human intervention and review. Although data elements can be moved relatively easily from one format to another by computer program, more complex formats like MARC do not currently offer data elements that can be used to carry fields that typically occur in the simpler formats, such as a generic (either corporate or personal) author without differentiation.

Roles for Automatic Indexing

Automatic (algorithmically based, computerized) indexing has been proposed—largely by people outside the library community—as a more powerful and simultaneously more cost-effective alternative to traditional bibliographic description and classification since the 1960s. Several different approaches to automatic indexing and classification have been explored by the research community, ranging from the primarily statistical approaches championed by Gerald Salton and his colleagues to methods based on natural-language processing.

There has been an ongoing debate about the quality of these techniques, a debate that has been problematic for a number of reasons. One cannot consider indexing methods in the abstract; their effectiveness has to be measured in the context of their use within some retrieval system. The typical comparison has been between automatic indexing approaches and simple keyword indexing and Boolean keyword retrieval for full-text documents; it has not usually been a comparison between automatic indexing of full-text documents (or their abstracts) on the one hand and the use of bibliographic records describing them within an online catalog on the other. In addition, until well into the 1990s, virtually all studies of automatic indexing relied on unrealistically small corpora of material, such as the Cranfield collections, rather than real-world databases. It was not until the TIPSTER and TREC experiments that these algorithms began to be validated with realistic databases of material. There are also some technical problems with statistically based automatic indexing of documents. The indexing is typically computed for a document in the context of a specific document collection, and thus cannot be interchanged as a surrogate for the document (relatively independently of context) in the same way that bibliographic descriptions can. A bibliographic description is relatively independent of its document's context (except for shelf-position information in the call number; subject schemes are also not universal, but are common to classes of collections rather than to specific collections).

Leaving aside the very real questions about the quality and robustness of computer-based indexing algorithms (as compared with human cataloging and classification), one serious practical objection to the automatic indexing approach has been the lack of availability of primary electronic content to be indexed. Only in rare cases (such as LEXIS and WESTLAW) have large amounts of full text been available to support use of automatic indexing algorithms. This has recently begun to change drastically with the widespread availability of full-text materials on the World Wide Web. Indeed, in the Web environment full-text documents appear first, and indexing and retrieval systems follow the availability of the documents. This is very different from the assumptions that underlie bibliographic systems designed to manage physical rather than electronic content.

Recently there have been serious efforts to extend automatic indexing approaches to multimedia content—images, audio, and video—that have resisted any type of economically viable large-scale cataloging. The automatic indexing approaches have not attempted to address some of the most problematic cataloging issues, such as contending with the many levels of meaning in images (iconographic interpretation); however, they are beginning to be able to answer queries such as "find images with many small yellow patches in a field of green," queries not addressed by traditional descriptive and subject cataloging. These developments point toward an environment where at the very least we can expect to find computationally derived metadata associated with digital objects that may well be distinct from but complementary to traditional descriptive and subject cataloging.

Intellectual property issues are poorly explored in connection with automatic indexing, and these may prove to have a significant influence on its future role. Typically, a record containing descriptive and subject cataloging is not considered a derivative work; it is considered either to be uncopyrighted (a simple collection of facts) or to have separate, independent status as intellectual property distinct from the work that it describes. Most rights-holders have not objected to the creation of cataloging for their work and, indeed, if the cataloger can legitimately obtain access to a copy of the work (for example, by purchasing or borrowing a copy of a physical work within the scope of the doctrine of First Sale and the regime of copyright), the rights-holder has no real legal basis, to the best of my knowledge, for preventing the creation of a descriptive record. For automatic indexing, the indexing program must be able to process the electronic form of the work, which normally means (except for the sort of publicly available material that is typically found on the Web today) that this must be explicitly permitted as a legitimate use under a license agreement governing the use of the electronic content. Arguably, the output of the automatic indexing program might well be considered a derivative work, and thus one over which the rights-holder of the object being described continues to have legal control. Thus, representations of objects that are created through automatic indexing may not be able to be used and interchanged freely and independently of the works that they describe, unlike traditional bibliographic descriptions. Further complicating the picture, many of the most sophisticated automatic indexing algorithms are viewed as proprietary by their authors, who may place restrictions on the use of indexing results produced by their algorithms.

There seems to be little question, in a time of continually diminishing costs for computational resources, that automatic indexing is likely to be less costly than traditional cataloging. For some classes of electronic information, particularly relatively ephemeral or low-value information, it seems virtually certain that automatic indexing will be the only realistic option. For other material, intellectual indexing, at the level of either traditional cataloging or one of the simplified descriptive schemes discussed earlier, is clearly reasonable and cost-justified. There is a vast middle ground, and we have a very poor understanding of the cost trade-offs and the decision-making criteria for employing one approach over the other. We also do not understand well how to integrate the two approaches in description support or retrieval systems. This gap in our understanding—and indeed the perception of intellectual description and automatic indexing as opposite, competing approaches each with its own advocates—is emphasized by the fact that we do not have interchange formats for describing works that effectively combine the results of automatic indexing algorithms and intellectual description.

Surrogates and the Objects That They Describe

Traditional cataloging practice is based on several fundamental assumptions that are increasingly coming into question. Historically there has been a fairly clear idea of when two objects are the same, in the sense that they would receive the same cataloging within similar contexts (that is, a common choice of subject classification scheme and of authorities). The easy ability to reformat content across media has already raised some doubts in the cataloging community: Is a version of a film on a VCR cassette really that different from the same film on 35mm film stock? Does it really make sense to distinguish paperbound and hardbound versions of the same book, assuming that they have identical content and pagination, just because of the binding? Should these differing formats of the same content justify distinct bibliographic records, or should cataloging begin to introduce the notion of a record that can describe several presumably insignificant variations in the physical packaging of the same intellectual content?

At the same time, we find the notion that there is, in traditional cataloging, something close to a canonical bibliographic description of an object, given choices about authorities and subject classification schemes to be used to describe it. One can think about a single master surrogate record that is used to describe an object.

In the world of digital information, equivalence of two objects is quickly becoming a very delicate matter, as information can be reformatted from one form to another, with all manner of subtle impacts on the integrity and reversibility of the transformation due to encoding, representation, and compression schemes. How different are SGML, ASCII, and bitmapped representations of a document, or JPEG and GIF versions of an image?

In this new digital world we find that equivalence of objects is contextual, subjective, situational, and hierarchical (in the sense that objects may differ in detail while being identical at some higher level of abstraction). At the lowest, most literal level we can consider two objects as identical only if they are exactly the same set of sequences of bits. More abstract concepts of identical objects may span different formats. Some may be even more liberal than the rules that normally are used in traditional bibliographic description, overlooking the details of separate editions and recognizing works at a very gross level of intellectual content. The linkage between instances of objects at various levels of abstraction and the surrogate records that describe them (however these surrogates are produced) will be captured through linkage mechanisms such as Uniform Resource Names. The relative nature of the equality of two instances of an object is captured in the naming rules that individual naming authorities will define and implement. Two objects may be the same (have the same name) in the eyes of one naming authority and be distinct (have different names) in the eyes of another.

There is, I believe, a growing (albeit still uneasy) consensus about the necessity for a relativistic view of identity and equivalence for digital objects. This is at odds, in a very fundamental way, with much of the view that we have of print publishing (though the largely unaddressed reality is that practices such as micro-editions that have emerged in the print-publishing world over the past few decades have undermined our certainties about when two printed works are treated identically for the purposes of description or citation). Views of, and approaches to, bibliographic description in the networked information environment will have to become sufficiently flexible to accommodate these ambiguities about the equivalence of objects being described in different contexts.

Ultimately, I would speculate that this loss of certainty may have a liberating effect both on description—permitting it to become more closely adapted to the varying contexts of user needs rather than some absolute view of bibliographic "reality" or "truth"—and on the ability of retrieval systems to match the needs of users in an environment characterized by an increasing richness of information.

Consider the mundane and simple case (compared with the evolving networked information environment) of a large online catalog describing printed works. When one retrieves all the works of a prolifically published author such as Shakespeare, one often wants to be able to control the level of abstraction at which the result set is displayed. For example, one might want to start an examination of the result set by viewing only the major works (without regard to specific editions or other detailed variations). One might then navigate to a specific work and examine the details of variant editions and versions of that work. Although some provocative experiments in this area have been carried out by groups like the OCLC Office of Research, this idea of dynamically controlled levels of abstraction has not reached the mainstream of retrieval systems. I suspect that it will become essential in the networked information environment and, in the interests of consistency, will also be extended backward to bibliographic databases describing primarily printed works, to the great benefit of users of these systems.

Metadata and New Types of Description and Classification: The Broader Picture

As already discussed, it seems likely that there will be a multiplicity of legitimate bibliographic descriptions of digital objects at varying levels of abstraction. The digital environment introduces a range of other new demands as well. It is clear that objects in the digital environment need to be managed in a much more active and complex way than printed artifacts. Metadata will need to be associated with objects to facilitate this management. Further, the digital environment is being held to a much higher standard, both by legislative mandate and by user suspicion, than the print-publishing world. It seems likely, for example, that the networked information environment will need to filter the transport and delivery of objects based on such criteria as sex and violence ratings. Although in the print realm readers seem prepared to assume that a plausible-looking document that claims to be written by a certain author and distributed by a certain publisher is what it seems to be, there is a demand in the digital environment that objects be accompanied by metadata that permit proof of authorship and provenance.

In the networked information environment, the following are some of the classes of metadata that may need to accompany a digital object or be associated with that object as independent surrogate records (with separate status as independently owned and managed intellectual property in some cases):

Description. This may include traditional descriptive and subject cataloging, discipline-specific description and cataloging (for example, for geospatial data), or the new lower-quality descriptions discussed earlier.

Advertising.

Rights and permissions information that describes who may have access to the object, what use they may make of it, and the costs of such use.

Security information.

Authentication information that allows the origin and chain of evidence of the object to be established.

Integrity and provenance information, which tracks the transformations that have been applied to the object since its initial canonical publication form and the effects that these transformations have had on the object's integrity.

Reviews and evaluative information.

Labels, such as PICS systems labels for reading level and sex and violence content.

Impact factors, based, for example, on how often the object has been cited or otherwise referenced, or perhaps on frequency of use.

Follow-up work to the Dublin Core definition at the Warwick Metadata Workshop in April 1996 underscored the need to accommodate the full scope of classes of metadata associated with digital objects in order to arrive at implementable solutions for managing and providing access to such objects. It was repeatedly emphasized that just supporting descriptive cataloging was not sufficient.

All these different types of metadata may come from different sources. They will likely have different formats. They may be independently owned. They will apply at different levels of abstraction. There is an urgent need (which the report of the Warwick meeting begins to address) for broad container formats to allow the arbitrary packaging of these various classes of metadata. It should be clear that "metadata" is not simply a new, more prestigious term for descriptive and subject cataloging. Traditional bibliographic description is only a small part of the broad range of metadata needed to support the discovery, retrieval, use, and management of digital objects. It should also be clear that these fundamentally new types of metadata are not simply incremental extensions of the descriptive and subject cataloging tradition, and that it is unlikely that they can be incrementally incorporated into the interchange formats that have been developed in support of traditional cataloging. They will not fit gracefully as additional fields in a MARC record, for example. Rather, MARC/AACR2 records are likely to be one of a range of classes of metadata that will be encapsulated and carried in the broader container formats that are now being proposed and developed.

Conclusion: Rethinking Objectives for an Economy of Scarce Attention

When one looks at the development of the next generations of descriptive and subject cataloging rules and practices, one can see, I believe, two overarching issues.

The first is that user needs are changing. Cataloging was originally established to support the management of physical objects and retrieval of surrogates for objects (through card catalogs, most commonly). These surrogates led the user to objects based on a set of criteria that assumed that information was a scarce resource. The goals of catalogs as articulated 50 or 75 years ago are still relevant to some user needs, but perhaps to an increasingly small and specialized set of these needs. The transition from card catalogs to online catalogs was accomplished based on available (bibliographic) data, without any fundamental reassessment of whether the descriptive data being produced by the cataloging process continued to be responsive to user needs. The best of today's online catalogs are vastly superior to card catalogs. However, their functional extensions are opportunistic, based again on available data and the ability of current computational resources to use these data as retrieval criteria, rather than on a rigorous rethinking of retrieval functionality based on user requirements. Even in large online catalogs it is clear that, while these systems can provide exhaustive, large results in response to user queries, they cannot answer questions that ask them to identify a "few good books" or, even more difficult, "where to spend the four hours I have available to read up on a topic." Such queries are increasingly of central importance to a growing number of users.

Several authors have suggested that we are moving into an environment where attention, rather than information, is the scarce resource: There is too much relevant information. Current practices provide little help in developing databases that can be responsive to queries within the context of an "economics of attention" rather than information. The networked information discovery and retrieval problem on the Internet, the need to identify appropriate information services within which searches can be pursued fruitfully (in other words, the multistage search model where one first identifies sources of answers and then interacts with these sources to obtain the desired answers that are the ultimate goal), and the need to understand the integration of collaborative/community information-filtering technologies into retrieval systems all highlight problems with current descriptive practice as an effective response to user requirements.

Meeting real user needs in the new electronic information environment will require not only a rethinking of cataloging practice but also an acceptance of the fact that the tradition of cataloging alone cannot address the full range of user needs. Cataloging information will need to be augmented and complemented by a wide range of other metadata from a variety of sources, and approaches will need to be developed that effectively combine the full array of information about digital objects.

The second overarching issue is the changing nature of digital information objects. The discussion in this chapter has focused on what Stuart

Weibel has termed "document-like" objects. These are objects that fit relatively comfortably within the intellectual framework of descriptive cataloging as it is currently practiced. In fact, the array of digital information that will be available goes far beyond this class of objects to encompass dynamically evolving databases, continuous video, telemetry and sensor feeds, and traces of communications and collaborative activities with very complex social and temporal dimensions such as newsgroups and data-analysis environments. It is not clear that these are most effectively described by analogy to the sorts of fixed print documents or serial publications that are the focus of current descriptive cataloging practices. These new genres of communication and discourse call for a fundamental reassessment of descriptive approaches based on user needs for identifying and retrieving information resources in the new networked information environment and the new economy of scarce attention. These new classes of digital objects invite us to develop new cooperative and complementary frameworks for automated, computer-based classification and indexing and intellectual analysis.

Bibliography

Alan, Robert. 1993. "Linking Successive Entries Based upon the OCLC Control Number, ISSN, or LCCN." *Library Resources & Technical Services* 37(4): 403–13.

Allen, Thelma E., and Daryl Ann Dickman, eds. 1967. *New Rules for an Old Game: Proceedings of a Workshop on the 1967 Anglo-American Cataloging Code Held at the School of Librarianship, the University of British Columbia, April 13 and 14, 1967.* Vancouver, B.C.: Publications Centre, University of British Columbia.

American Library Association, Association for Library Collections & Technical Services, Cataloging and Classification Section, Committee on Cataloging: Description and Access, Task Force to Review Reproduction Cataloging Guidelines. 1993. "Final Report."

Anglo-American Cataloging Rules. North American Text. 1967. Chicago: American Library Association.

Anglo-American Cataloguing Rules, 2d ed., 1988 Revision. 1988. Chicago: American Library Association.

Atkinson, Ross. 1995. "Humanities Scholarship and the Research Library." *Library Resources & Technical Services* 39(1): 79–84.

Attig, John. 1989. "Descriptive Cataloging Rules and Machine-Readable Record Structures: Some Directions for Parallel Development." In *The Conceptual Foundations of Descriptive Cataloging,* edited by Elaine Svenonius, 135–48. San Diego: Academic Press.

Barnes, Susan, and Janet McCue. 1991. "Linking Library Records to Bibliographic Databases: An Analysis of Common Data Elements in BIOSIS, Agricola, and the OPAC." *Cataloging & Classification Quarterly* 13(3/4): 157–87.

Bartley, Linda, Julia Blixrud, and Maureen Landry. 1990. "LiOnCat: The Library Online Catalog (with a Focus on Serials)." Unpublished paper.

Beatty, Alison, and Betsy L. Humphreys. 1983. "Serial Cataloging Under AACR2: Differences and Difficulties at the National Library of Medicine." *Cataloging & Classification Quarterly* 3(2/3): 77–85.

[Beck], Melissa M. Bernhardt. 1988. "Dealing with Serial Title Changes: Some Theoretical and Practical Considerations." *Cataloging & Classification Quarterly* 9(2): 25–39.

Bross, Rex. 1992. "Saved by the Uniform Title: Would AACR2 Have Worked for Serials without It?" In *Serials Cataloging: Modern Perspectives and International Developments*, edited by Jim E. Cole and James W. Williams, 123–26. Binghamton, N.Y.: Haworth Press. Also published in *Serials Librarian* 22 (1992): 123–26.

Butler, Todd. 1992. "Sex, Lies, and Newspapers: The Newspaper Cataloging and Union Listing Manual." In *Serials Cataloging*, 165–82. Also published in *Serials Librarian* 22 (1992): 165–82.

Callahan, Patrick F. 1992. "ISBD(S) Revised Edition and AACR2 1988 Revision: A Comparison." In *Serials Cataloging*, 249–62. Also published in *Serials Librarian* 22 (1992): 249–62.

Carpenter, Michael, and Elaine Svenonius, eds. 1985. *Foundations of Cataloging: A Sourcebook*. Littleton, Colo.: Libraries Unlimited.

Chartier, Roger. 1994. *The Order of Books: Readers, Authors, and Libraries in Europe between the Fourteenth and Eighteenth Centuries*. Stanford, Calif.: Stanford University Press.

Clack, Doris Hargrett, ed. 1980. *The Making of a Code: The Issues Underlying AACR2: Papers Given at the International Conference on AACR2 held March 11–14, 1979, in Tallahassee, Florida*. Chicago: American Library Association.

Cole, Jim E., and James W. Williams, eds. 1992. *Serials Cataloging: Modern Perspectives and International Developments*. Binghamton, N.Y.: Haworth Press. Also published as *Serials Librarian* 22 (1992).

Cooperative Online Serials Program. 1993. *CONSER Cataloging Manual*, edited by Jean Hirons. Washington, D.C.: Library of Congress, Cataloging Distribution Service.

———. 1994. *CONSER Editing Guide*. 1994 ed. Washington, D.C.: Library of Congress, Cataloging Distribution Service.

Cutter, Charles A. 1904. *Rules for a Dictionary Catalog*. 4th ed., rewritten. Washington, D.C.: Government Printing Office.

Delsey, Tom. 1989. "Authority Control in an International Context." In *Authority Control in the Online Environment: Considerations and Practices,* edited by Barbara B. Tillett, 13–28. New York: Haworth Press. Also published in *Cataloging & Classification Quarterly* 9 (1989): 3.

Dreyfus, Hubert L. 1992. *What Computers Still Can't Do: A Critique of Artificial Reason.* Cambridge, Mass.: MIT Press.

Duke, John K. 1983. "AACR2 Serial Records and the User." *Cataloging & Classification Quarterly* 3(2/3): 111–17.

Edgar, Neal L. 1980. "Impact of AACR2 on Serials and Analysis." In *The Making of a Code,* 88–105.

Fetzer, James H. 1990. *Artificial Intelligence: Its Scope and Limits.* Studies in Cognitive Systems, vol. 4. Dordrecht, Netherlands: Kluwer Academic Publishers.

"Future Directions for the Cataloging Rules Meeting." 1994. "Notes from an informal, non-official creativity/brainstorming meeting, Los Angeles, CA, Figueroa Hotel, Sunday, February 6, 1994." Compiled, with introductory notes, by Laurel Jizba. Typescript. East Lansing, Mich.: Michigan State University Libraries.

Gorman, Michael. 1992. "After AACR2R: The Future of the Anglo-American Cataloguing Rules." In *Origins, Content, and Future of AACR2 Revised,* edited by Richard Smiraglia, 89–94. ALCTS Papers on Library Technical Services and Collections, no. 2. Chicago: American Library Association.

———. 1978. "The Anglo-American Cataloguing Rules, Second Edition." *Library Resources & Technical Services,* 22(3): 209–26.

———. 1982. "Authority Control in the Prospective Catalog." In *Authority Control: The Key to Tomorrow's Catalog; Proceedings of the 1979 Library and Information Technology Association Institutes,* edited by Mary W. Ghikas, 166–80. Phoenix, Ariz.: Oryx Press.

Gorman, Michael, and Robert H. Burger. 1980. "Serial Control in a Developed Machine System." *Serials Librarian* 5(1): 13–26.

Graham, Crystal. 1992. "Microform Reproductions and Multiple Versions." In *Serials Cataloging,* 213–34. Also published in *Serials Librarian* 22 (1992): 213–14.

Gregor, Dorothy, and Carol Mandel. 1991. "Cataloging Must Change!" *Library Journal* 116(6): 42–47.

Guidelines for Bibliographic Description of Reproductions. 1995. Chicago: Association for Library Collections & Technical Services.

Hallam, Adele. 1992. *Cataloging Rules for the Description of Looseleaf Publications.* 2d ed. Washington, D.C.: Library of Congress, Cataloging Distribution Service.

Haworth, Kent M. 1993. "The Voyage of *RAD:* From the Old World to the New." *Archivaria* 35 (Spring): 55–63.

Henderson, Kathryn Luther. 1992. "Personalities of Their Own: Some Informal Thoughts on Serials and Teaching about How to Catalog Them." In *Serials Cataloging,* 3–16. Also published in *Serials Librarian* 22 (1992): 3–16.

Hensen, Steven L. 1994. "APPM and American Description Standards in Relation to ISAD(G)." Paper delivered at International Seminar on Standards for Archival Description of European Archives: Experience and Proposals, San Miniato, Italy, August 1994. (Forthcoming in *Archivi & Computer.*)

———. 1983. *Archives, Personal Papers, and Manuscripts: A Cataloging Manual for Archival Repositories, Historical Societies, and Manuscript Libraries.* Washington, D.C.: Library of Congress.

———. 1990. *Archives, Personal Papers, and Manuscripts: A Cataloging Manual for Archival Repositories, Historical Societies, and Manuscript Libraries.* 2d ed. Chicago: Society of American Archivists.

———. 1993. "The First Shall Be Last: *APPM* and Its Impact on American Archival Description." *Archivaria* 35 (Spring): 64–70.

Hjerppe, Roland, and Birgitta Olander. "Cataloging and Expert Systems: AACR2 as a Knowledge Base." *Journal of the American Society for Information Science* 40(1): 27–44.

Howarth, Lynne C., and Jean Weihs. 1994. "*AACR2R:* Dissemination and Use in Canadian Libraries." *Library Resources & Technical Services* 38(2): 179–89.

International Conference on Cataloguing Principles. 1963. *Report: International Conference on Cataloguing Principles, Paris, 9th–18th October, 1961.* London: Organizing Committee of the International Conference on Cataloguing Principles.

———. 1971. *Statement of Principles,* adopted at the International Conference on Cataloguing Principles, Paris, October, 1961. Annotated ed., with commentary and examples by Eva Verona, assisted by Franz

Georg Kaltwasser, P. R. Lewis, and Roger Pierrot. London: IFLA Committee on Cataloguing.

International Federation of Library Associations. 1969, c1963. *International Conference on Cataloguing Principles, Paris, 9th–18th October, 1961: Report,* edited by A. H. Chaplin and Dorothy Anderson. London: Clive Bingley on behalf of IFLA.

Kelly, John. 1993. *Artificial Intelligence: A Modern Myth.* Ellis Horwood Series in Artificial Intelligence. New York: Ellis Horwood.

Kilgour, Frederick G. 1995. "Effectiveness of Surname-Title-Words Searches by Scholars." *Journal of the American Society for Information Science* 46(2): 145–51.

Leathem, Cecilia A. 1994. "An Examination of Choice of Formats for Cataloging Nontextual Serials." *Serials Review* 20(5): 59–67.

Leazer, Gregory H. 1992. "An Examination of Data Elements for Bibliographic Description: Toward a Conceptual Schema for the USMARC Formats." *Library Resources & Technical Services* 36(2): 189–208.

Levy, David M. 1995. "Cataloging in the Digital Order." In *Proceedings of Digital Libraries '95: The Second Annual Conference on the Theory and Practice of Digital Libraries, June 11–13, 1995, Austin, Texas,* edited by Frank M. Shipman, Richard Furuta, and David M. Levy, 31–37. College Station, Tex.: Hypermedia Research Laboratory.

———. 1994. "Fixed or Fluid?: Document Stability and New Media." In *European Conference on Hypermedia Technology, 1994: Proceedings,* 24–31. New York: Association for Computing Machinery.

———. 1995. "Naming the Nameable: Names, Versions, and Document Identity in a Networked Environment." In *Scholarly Publishing on the Electronic Networks: Filling the Pipeline and Paying the Piper: Proceedings of the Fourth Symposium: November 5–7, 1994, the Washington Vista Hotel, Washington, D.C.,* edited by Ann Okerson, 153–59. Washington, D.C.: Association of Research Libraries.

———. 1992. "What Do You See and What Do You Get? Document Identity and Electronic Media." In *Screening Words: User Interfaces for Text. Proceedings of the Eighth Annual Conference of the UW Centre for the New OED and Text Research,* 109–17. Waterloo, Ont.: UW Centre for the New OED and Text Research.

Library of Congress. 1990. *Library of Congress Rule Interpretations.* 2d ed. Washington, D.C.: Library of Congress, Cataloging Distribution Service.

———. 1992 (revised 1994). "Report of the IE Analysis Project Team." Typescript.

———. 1993. *USMARC Format for Authority Data.* Washington, D.C.: Library of Congress, Cataloging Distribution Service.

Lubetzky, Seymour. 1953. *Cataloging Rules and Principles.* Washington, D.C.: Processing Department, Library of Congress.

———. 1960. *Code of Cataloging Rules: Author and Title Entry.* "Unfinished draft for a new edition of cataloging rules, prepared for the Catalog Code Revision Committee; with an explanatory commentary by Paul Dunkin." [Chicago]: American Library Association.

———. 1969. *Principles of Cataloging.* Los Angeles: Institute of Library Research, University of California.

Malinconico, S. Michael. 1980. "AACR and Automation." In *The Making of a Code,* 25–40.

Manley, Will. 1994. "Catalogers, We Hardly Know Ye." *American Libraries* 25(7): 661.

Multiple Versions Forum. 1990. *Multiple Versions Forum Report: Report from a Meeting Held December 6–8, 1989, Airlie, Virginia.* Washington, D.C.: Network Development and MARC Standards Office, Library of Congress.

Nunberg, Geoffrey D. 1993. "The Places of Books in the Age of Electronic Reproduction." *Representations* 42: 13–37.

Packer, Katherine H., and Delores Phillips, eds. c1969. *The Code and the Cataloguer: Proceedings of the Colloquium on the Anglo-American Cataloging Rules, Held at the School of Library Science, University of Toronto on March 31 and April 1, 1967.* Toronto, Ont.: University of Toronto Press.

Reynolds, Regina. 1995. "Paper and Beyond: Cataloging the Evolving Serial." Paper presented at the Association of Library Collections and Technical Services Serials Cataloging in the Age of Format Integration Institute, April 7, 1995, Atlanta.

Ristad, Eric Sven. 1993. *The Language Complexity Game.* Artificial Intelligence. Cambridge, Mass.: MIT Press.

Rose, M. 1993. *Authors and Owners: The Invention of Copyright.* Cambridge, Mass.: Harvard University Press.

Rosenberg, Frieda B. 1996. "Cataloging Serials." In *Serials Management,* edited by Marcia Tuttle, 195–234. Foundations in Library and Information Science, vol. 35. Greenwich, Conn.: JAI Press.

Rychlak, Joseph F. 1991. *Artificial Intelligence and Human Reason: A Teleological Critique.* New York: Columbia University Press.

Suchman, Lucy. 1995. "Making Work Visible." *Communications of the ACM* 38(9): 56–64.

Svenonius, Elaine, ed. 1989. *The Conceptual Foundations of Descriptive Cataloging.* San Diego, Calif.: Academic Press.

Tillett, Barbara B. 1990. "Access Control: A Model for Descriptive, Holding, and Control Records." In *Convergence: Proceedings of the Second National Conference of the Library and Information Technology Association, October 2–6, 1988, Boston, Massachusetts,* edited by Michael Gorman, 48–56. Chicago: American Library Association.

―――. 1992. "Bibliographic Relationships: An Empirical Study of the LC Machine-Readable Records." *Library Resources & Technical Services* 36(2): 162–88.

―――. 1987. *Bibliographic Relationships: Toward a Conceptual Structure of Bibliographic Information Used in Cataloging.* Ph.D. Dissertation. Los Angeles: University of California, Los Angeles.

―――. 1992. "The History of Linking Devices." *Library Resources & Technical Services* 36(1): 23–36.

―――. 1985. "1984 Automated Authority Control Opinion Poll: A Preliminary Analysis." *Information Technology and Libraries* 4 (June): 171–78.

―――. 1991. "A Summary of the Treatment of Bibliographic Relationships in Cataloging Rules." *Library Resources & Technical Services* 35(4): 393–405.

―――. 1991. "A Taxonomy of Bibliographic Relationships." *Library Resources & Technical Services* 35(2): 150–58.

Weihs, Jean, and Lynne C. Howarth. 1995. "Nonbook Materials: Their Occurrence and Bibliographic Description in Canadian Libraries." *Library Resources & Technical Services* 39(2): 184–97.

Willard, Louis Charles. 1981. "Microforms and AACR2, Chapter 11: Is the Cardinal Principle a Peter Principle?" *Microform Review* 10(2): 75–78.

Wool, Gregory J., et al. 1993. "Cataloging Standards and Machine Translation: A Study of Reformatted ISBD Records in an Online Catalog." *Information Technology and Libraries* 12(4): 383–403.

Yee, Martha M. 1993. "The Concept of *Work* for Moving Image Materials." *Cataloging & Classification Quarterly* 18(2): 33–40.

———. 1994. "Manifestations and Near-Equivalents: Theory, with Special Attention to Moving-Image Materials." *Library Resources & Technical Services* 38(3): 227–55.

———. 1994. "Manifestations and Near-Equivalents of Moving Image Works: A Research Project." *Library Resources & Technical Services* 38(4): 355–72.

———. 1991. "System Design and Cataloging Meet the User: User Interfaces to Online Public Access Catalogs." *Journal of the American Society for Information Science* 42(2): 78–96.

———. 1994. "What Is a Work? Part 1, The User and the Objects of the Catalog." *Cataloging & Classification Quarterly* 19(1): 9–28.

———. 1994. "What Is a Work? Part 2, The Anglo-American Cataloging Codes." *Cataloging & Classification Quarterly* 19(2): 5–22.

———. 1995. "What Is a Work? Part 3, The Anglo-American Cataloging Codes, Continued." *Cataloging & Classification Quarterly* 20(1): 25–46.

———. 1995. "What Is a Work? Part 4, Cataloging Theorists and a Definition." *Cataloging & Classification Quarterly* 20(2): 3–24.

Acronyms and Initialisms Used

AA 1908	Catalog Rules, Author and Title Entries
AACR	Anglo-American Cataloguing Rules
AACR1	Anglo-American Cataloging Rules, first edition (1967)
AACR2	Anglo-American Cataloguing Rules, second edition (1978; revised 1988, and amended 1993)
ALA 1949	A.L.A. Cataloging Rules for Author and Title Entries
ARPA	Advanced Research Projects Agency
ASCII	American Standard Code for Information Interchange
DDC	Dewey Decimal Classification
DTD	Document Type Definition
GIF	Graphics Interchange Format
HTML	HyperText Markup Language
IFLA	International Federation of Library Associations and Institutions
ISBD	International Standard Bibliographic Description
ISBN	International Standard Book Number
ISSN	International Standard Serial Number
JPEG	Joint Photographic Experts Group
JSC	Joint Steering Committee for Revision of AACR
LC	Library of Congress
LCC	Library of Congress Classification

LCRI	Library of Congress Rule Interpretations
LCSH	Library of Congress Subject Headings
MARC	MAchine-Readable Cataloging
MARC AMC	MAchine-Readable Cataloging, Archives and Manuscript Control
NIDR	Networked Information Discovery and Retrieval
NISTF	National Information Systems Task Force
OCLC	OCLC Online Computer Library Center, Inc.
OPAC	Online Public Access Catalog
PCC	Program for Cooperative Cataloging
RLG	Research Library Group
SGML	Standard Generalized Markup Language
TEI	Text Encoding Initiative
UBC	Universal Bibliographic Control
URC	Uniform Resource Characteristic
URL	Uniform Resource Locator
URN	Uniform Resource Name

Index

AACR1 (Anglo-American Cataloging Rules), 10–12
AACR2, 109
  and archives, 86
  and authority control, 31–32
  and editions, 41
  history, 12–15
  as major change, 24–25
  serials, 66–83
  uniform titles, 34
AACR2 Chapter 12, 71
AACR2 Chapter 25, 34
AACR2 Rule 0.5, 31–32, 33
AACR2 Rule 0.24, 68, 71
AACR2 Rule 21.1, 74
AACR2 Rule 26.0, 31–32, 33
access control records, 38
access points, 94
  in AACR2, 24–25
  in online catalogs, 32–33
  uncontrolled, 111
accuracy, 7
added entries
  serial titles, 77
  uniting editions, 53
advertising, 117
A.L.A. *Cataloging Rules for Author and Title Entries* ("red book"), 23
alternative rules in AACR2, 14
Anglo-American Authority File, 37, 38
Anglo-American Cataloging Rules (AACR1), 10–12
Anglo-American Cataloguing Code. *See* AACR2

APPM *(Archives, Personal Papers, and Manuscripts)*, 86–87
archives, 84–96
Archives, Personal Papers, and Manuscripts, 86–87
arrangement of bibliographic records, 39
artificial intelligence, 53
ASN.1 structures, 109
authentication information, 117
authority control, 30–39
authority files, 33
  in AACR3, 28
  and shared cataloging, 53
authors
  in AACR2, 25
  and electronic distribution, 43–44
  identification, 31
automatic indexing, 111, 112–14

backlogs, 95. *See also* Timeliness
bibliographic attributes, 36
bibliographic description
  digital materials, 107–20
  of metadata, 117
  serials, 69–70
bibliographic relationships, 36
boundaries of materials, 101, 103

card catalogs, 78, 95
  and authority control, 32
catalog records
  digitized, 102
  serials, 67–68

catalogers, 98–100
cataloging codes, 6–18
Cataloging Rules for the Description of Looseleaf Publications, 73
catalogs, 54–55, 119
  authority control in, 30–31
  and editions, 45
  certainty in bibliographic description, 116
chained added entries, 53
change in digital materials, 101
change in editions, 42
changes in imprint for serials, 69
choice of entry for serials, 74
citation form, 39
computer files, 71–72
Computer Science Technical Report project, 111
CONSER Cataloging Manual, 69, 78
CONSER Editing Guide, 69
consistency
  in AACR2, 68
  Cutter on, 7
  and Paris Principles, 11
content change, 42
content labels, 118
controlled access, 35–36, 37. *See also* Subject access
cooperative cataloging, 53, 54–55, 78
copies, 41
copyright, 113–14
corporate bodies
  in AACR1, 11
  serials, 74, 75
Cutter, Charles, 7, 45
  and authority control, 30

depth of cataloging, 111–12
descriptive cataloging
  and AACR2, 14
  objectives of, 44–45
differences significant to users, 42
digital information objects, 117–20
digital materials, 97–106, 107–20. *See also* Electronic resources
Dublin Core Metadata set, 111, 118

Duke University backlog (Guido Mazzoni Collection), 92–94

economics of attention, 119
editions, 40–65, 41
electronic distribution, 43
electronic resources, 21–23, 28. *See also* Digital materials
electronic serials, 71–72
e-mail discussion groups, 16
evaluative information, 117
extent of change, 42
extent of item, 44

Federal Geographic Data Committee metadata format, 110
filters, 117
finding aids, 90
flexibility of AACR2, 27
flowcharts, 80
fonds, 89
Form and Structure of Corporate Headings, 37
form headings, 34
  and AACR2, 13
formats as different entities, 115. *See also* Near-equivalents
frequency change, 77
fullness, 7, 8
full-text materials, 113
  online journals, 72

genres of digital materials, 101–2, 104
geographic names in IFLA guidelines, 37
"green book" *(Rules for Descriptive Cataloging),* 9
  relation to AACR1, 23
Guidelines for Bibliographic Description of Reproductions, 71
Guidelines for the Description of Reproductions, 46

hierarchical levels of works, 55
history, 6–18
holdings information, 67
home pages, 102
Hypertext Markup Language (HTML), 94

iconographic interpretations, 113
IFLA
  and bibliographic control, 37
  Study Group on Functional Requirements of Bibliographic Records, 35
impact factors, 118
imprint for serials, 69–70
Information Engineering Analysis Pilot Study Project, 90
integrated online systems
  serials in, 67
intellectual content of materials, 89, 90–92, 113
intellectual property and automatic indexing, 113–14
interchange formats, 109–10
International Conference on Cataloguing Principles, 9, 10. *See also* Paris Principles
International Standard Authority Number (ISAN), 38
International Standard for Bibliographic Description. *See* ISBD
International Standard Serial Number (ISSN), 68, 77
internationalization
  authority records, 36–38
Internet, 95
  and AACR2, 16
  access to, 21–23
  as delivery system, 88
  indexing, 113
  serials on, 72
inventory of materials, 91–92
ISAN (International Standard Authority Number), 38
ISBD (International Standard for Bibliographic Description), 26, 68

ISBD(G), 13–14, 24
ISBD(M), 13, 24
ISSN (International Standard Serial Number) System, 68
  and title changes, 77
  issuing bodies
    entry under, 74
    serials, 69

keyword access, 20, 111
Kilgour, Fred, 20–21

language change, 43
less-significant differences, 42, 43
Library of Congress Manuscript Division, 86
Library of Congress Rule Interpretations, 26, 28
  for editions, 46
  and serials, 69, 70
linked records for serials, 80
local system number, 80
location of materials, 89–90
looseleaf publications, 73
Lubetzky, Seymour, 8, 10, 45
  and AACR2, 23–24
  and authority control, 31

machine processing
  and AACR2, 13–14
  and descriptive cataloging, 16
  for serials, 75–76, 79
main entry, 16, 31–32
  in AACR1, 11
  in AACR2, 25
  in AACR3, 28
  in *Rules for Descriptive Cataloging,* 9
MARC AMC (USMARC format for archives and manuscript control), 85–86
MARC authority field 643, 70
MARC field 246, 74, 78
MARC field 260, 70
MARC field 362, 69

MARC field 510, 78
MARC field 550, 69
MARC field 76X-78X, 80
MARC format, 16, 26, 107, 109
  in AACR3, 28
  for authority records, 32
  as standard, 26
master record, 27
materiality of documents, 100, 103
metadata, 108
  AACR2 as packaging device for, 17
  in archival cataloging, 91, 94
microforms, 28. *See also* Multiple
  versions; Near-equivalents
multimedia content, 113
Multiple Database Access Service, 61
multiple versions, 70–71. *See also*
  Near-equivalents

Name Authority Cooperative Project, 37
Names of Persons, 37
National Coordinated Cataloging
  Program, 37
National Information Systems Task
  Force, 85–87
near-equivalents, 41, 46. *See also*
  Formats; Multiple versions
networked information discovery and
  retrieval, 108
nonbook materials in AACR2, 13
nonprint serials, 71

OCLC
  SiteSearch, 68
  standards, 20
online catalogs and authority control, 32
online databases, 73
Osborn, Andrew, 8
ownership and electronic distribution,
  43–44

Panizzi, Anthony, 6–7
Paris Principles, 10, 45
  and AACR1, 11

  and AACR2, 12, 13
  and archives, 88–89
permanence of digital materials, 101, 103
physical description
  archives, 89–90
  and electronic resources, 44
  for serials, 68
physical form of serials, 68
Program for Cooperative Cataloging, 37
provenance
  archives, 85
  of metadata, 117
publication information and electronic
  distribution, 43–44
punctuation, 79

record design, 54
"red book" *(A.L.A. Cataloging Rules for
  Author and Title Entries),* 23
references
  in authority records, 32
  in catalogs, 33
relationships between works, 55
reproductions, 46. *See also* Multiple
  versions; Near-equivalents
  and serials, 70–71
respect des fonds, 85, 93
reviews and evaluative information, 117
rights and permissions for metadata, 117
Rules for a Dictionary Catalog, 7
Rules for Descriptive Cataloging ("green
  book"), 9, 23

screen displays, 109
secondary materials, 102–4
security information, 117
serials, 66–83
series title change, 42
SGML Data Type Definitions, 109
SGML Document Type Definitions, 110
SGML (Standard Generalized Markup
  Language), 94, 109
shared cataloging. *See* Cooperative
  cataloging
simplification of rules, 26–27
special rules, 28

Standard Generalized Markup Language
  (SGML), 94, 109
standards, 20–21, 109
  and cooperative cataloging, 26
  statement of responsibility
    changes in, 42
    and serials, 69
strategic planning and cataloging, 27
subject access, 111. *See also* Controlled
    access
"super-work," 41–42
system design, 54

technology and authority control, 32–34
Text Encoding Initiative, 103, 110
timeliness, 111. *See also* Backlogs
TIPSTER experiment, 113
title added entries, 77
title changes, 75–77
  in serials, 53
  as significant difference, 42
transcription of data, 69
translations, 75
TREC experiment, 113

Uniform Resource Names, 104, 116
uniform titles, 34–35
  and AACR2, 13
  serials, 74–75
  uniting editions, 52–53

unique identifiers, 74
Universal Bibliographic Control, 14, 26, 37
unpublished materials, 28
usefulness, 7, 8
user expectations, 108, 119
  and Cutter, 7
USMARC format for archives and
  manuscript control (MARC AMC), 85–86
USMARC Format for Bibliographic Data, 69

variability of digital materials, 101
variant titles, 74, 77
Verona, Eva, 9
version, 41
virtual documents, 100
visual materials, 113

Warwick Metadata Workshop, 118
work, 41
Working Group on an International
  Authority System, 38
World Wide Web. *See* Internet
Worst Serial Title Changes, 76

Z39.2, 109